Great Australian
BEER YARNS

Great Australian
BEER YARNS

EDITED BY

Peter Lalor

ABC Books

The ABC 'Wave' device is a trademark of the Australian Broadcasting Corporation and is used under licence by HarperCollins*Publishers* Australia.

First published in Australia in 2002
This edition published in 2014
by HarperCollins*Publishers* Australia Pty Limited
ABN 36 009 913 517
harpercollins.com.au

Copyright for this collection and arrangement © Peter Lalor 2002, 2014
Copyright © and moral rights in individual stories remain with the contributors.

The right of Peter Lalor to be identified as the author of this work has been asserted by him in accordance with the *Copyright Amendment (Moral Rights) Act 2000*.

This work is copyright. Apart from any use as permitted under the *Copyright Act 1968*, no part may be reproduced, copied, scanned, stored in a retrieval system, recorded, or transmitted, in any form or by any means, without the prior written permission of the publisher.

HarperCollins*Publishers*
Level 13, 201 Elizabeth Street, Sydney NSW 2000, Australia
Unit D1, 63 Apollo Drive, Albany, Auckland 0632, New Zealand
A53, Sector 57, Noida, UP, India
77–85 Fulham Palace Road, London W6 8JB, United Kingdom
2 Bloor Street East, 20th floor, Toronto, Ontario M4W 1A8, Canada
10 East 53rd Street, New York NY 10022, USA

ISBN 978 0 7333 3327 9 (pbk)
ISBN 978 1 4607 0261 1 (ebook)

Cover design by HarperCollins Design Studio
Cover image: 'Bushfire fighters days later at a rigged up pub at Airey's Inlet'
© Rennie Ellis Photographic Archive
Internal image by shutterstock.com
Typeset in 10/15pt ITC Bookman by Kirby Jones
Printed and bound in Australia by Griffin Press
The papers used by HarperCollins in the manufacture of this book are a natural, recyclable product made from wood grown in sustainable plantation forests. The fibre source and manufacturing processes meet recognised international environmental standards, and carry certification.

5 4 3 2 1   14 15 16 17

He was a wise man who invented beer.

Plato

Contents

Contributors ix

YARNS

A Long Way to Tipperary 3 • A New Experience 8

A Thief's Hobby 9 • Aunt Bertha's Cure 10

Ballarat Bertie 13 • Bank Inspector 17

Banned From the Woodyard 18

Beer and Marriage 21 • Beer and Skittles 23

Beer Drench 25 • Black Days 26

Bogans and Beer 28 • Born in a Pub 30

Car Went the Old Way Home 31

Counting Sheep 33 • Crocket 34 • Curly 35

Drink Rider 36 • Ernie 37 • False Teeth 39

Fly in Beer 40 • Head Banger 42

Horse-pitell-ity 45 • How's About a Kiss? 47

Humpty Dummies 54 • I Saw the Light 56

It Ain't Heavy ... 58 • Medicinal Purposes 61

My Uncle 65 • Ouch 67

Praise God and Pass the VB 69

Schooner Grip 73 • Sinking a Beer 74

That Cocky's Dead 75 • The Lost Beers 78

There Is a God 79 • This One Looks Armless 82
Water Closet 86
Water Police, Warm Feet and a Beer Shower 88
Watering Down the Beer 91
Watering the Garden 94 • Wrong Number 95

FROTHY FACTS
A Sad End 99
Barmaid Bans and the Beer Uprising 101
Bob Hawke's Record 104
Breakfast of Champions 106
Cricketers 107 • Dead Drunk 115
Fishy Story 118 • Meaty Drop 120
Pub With No Beer 122 • Russia Ailed by Beer 124

WAR STORIES
A Bellyful 127 • A Case of VD 128
A Fosters or an Abbotts 129 • Beer Pyramid 130
Korean Hopsicles 132
Unopened Beer and Dunny Doors 135

HOME-BREWERS
A Beery Confession 141 • Bad Old Days 143
Cat-a-tonic 146 • Exploding Beer Bottles 149

Hard to Swallow 151 • Homies 155
Lollywater 158 • Mothballs 161 • Nightcap 163
Oh Dear, No Beer 165 • The Postie 167

AUSSIES ABROAD
A Blessed Life 171 • Blind Drunk 172
Collecting Glasses 174 • Colour Blind 177
For God's Sake 179 • Guinness for Mothers 180
On Parade 188 • Raskols 189
Russian Lights 191 • The Taste Test 194

JOKES 199

CONTRIBUTORS

June Benson
John Bogan
Kevin Bradley
Mark Bressington
Butch Brown
Paul Cairns
Louise Carr
Marcia Carr
Neil Chippendale
Kevin J Crouch
Mark Dennis
Bruce Dowling
Chris Dwyer
Paul Egan
Ken Evans
Fred Fortescue
John Gibbins
Glenn Gilbert
Neil Gillies
Hillary Greenup
James Hamilton
Ray Hardes
Terry Hayes
Kevin Hole
Chris Horneman
Jaak Jarv
Elaine Johnston
Bill Jones
Maurice Kealy
David Keane
Peter Lalor
Winston Lau
Paulene Lowe
Hayden MacKellar
Ray Mason
Andrew McCarthy
Barry McKiernan
Gerard Meares
Martin New
R T Noble
Brian Noyes
Lloyd O'Brien
Garry Phipps
Dudley C Pye

Jim Ratcliffe
Greg Rieper
Mike Sadler
Mrs E Shelley
Bernard Skitt
Carole Smith
Mary Smith
Paul Staunton
Peter Stehr
Ed Tonks

Penny Turner
Max van den Berg
Brian Wallace
Barry Williams
Garry Williamson
Norm Woodcock ...

... and many, many more

YARNS

A LONG WAY TO TIPPERARY
Mike Sadler

It was a hot day — a bloody hot day, in fact! We had been working the whole day on the mate's extensions — digging, levelling the dirt and mixing and pouring a tonne of concrete. Hot work. Thirsty work. It was getting late; the sun was well over the yardarm.

Mine host was a well-known tippler and so we had no fears that we would not be suitably rewarded for our sterling efforts on that day. Finally, it was time to down tools, stick our heads under the tap and hold out our hands in the time-honoured manner.

There is nothing like the expectation of an icy cold beer at the end of a long, hot day — and did we deserve it! (Has someone already said that?)

Our mate went to get the beers.

The minutes dragged on.

We'd heard the fridge open and close in the shed. What was he up to, slamming doors and that?

Then suddenly we heard curses, and the blue heeler, who'd been holed up in the cool of the shed, ran out yelping, followed by a cursing, spitting, red-faced bloke with murder in his eyes.

'Well, she's bloody done it this time!'

Dismayed, we listened and heard the sorry tale of last night's blue and his cringing appeasement that 'he really would give it up this time — no sweat'.

Of course, he didn't mean it, and had said the same thing many times, but nothing had ever come of it — who would take something like that seriously? The woman was obviously stark raving mad to empty a fridge full of grog on the one day when she knew he would need it and to replace it with bottles of water.

And to think we'd all said 'Bye' to her nicely when she drove off a few hours ago.

In a cupboard behind some motoring magazines he'd found a six-pack of fancy beer, left behind by some smarty at the big Hawaiian do we'd had a while ago (had a volcano at that one!). Even his teenage son — a chip off the old block if ever there was one — wouldn't come at it, so it had just sat there, gathering dust.

One of the blokes (he was a boy scout) chucked the water bottles onto the ground and shoved the six-pack into the remaining ice in the Esky, to take with us on the trip to the next house where, we were assured, there was a fridge full of grog just waiting for us.

Now, we are talking back in the bad old days here, when Sundays were as dry as a mother-in-law's kiss. The pubs were all shut.

Full of anticipation, we drove off chatting and laughing and hanging out for that cold one. We pulled up and strode confidently into his shed. He yanked the door open, talking over his shoulder to us, and I'll never forget his face when he saw the look on our faces as we saw inside. Shaking, he turned around and picked up the note from inside the empty fridge.

'She said you would come here. He needs help with his drinking, and so do you!'

A bit cheeky that, I thought.

So we piled back into the car and headed off to my place. The journey was made in grim silence. It was with a cold and sinking heart that I stopped in my drive. It was getting late by then and the house was shuttered and dark.

There was a faint glow from the shed at the back. We staggered like shipwrecked sailors towards the light.

She'd left the fridge door open and it wasn't until I'd wiped the tears from my eyes that I realised the note didn't say 'Up yours too' but 'You do too'.

Funny what a man's mind will do in extremis, isn't it?

Silently, Scout (we call him Scout now because of that night) went back to the car and handed us each a bottle of the foreign muck. The only word we could read on the label was 'Bier' and we had half an idea what that translated to.

We sat huddled in front of the open fridge, like worshippers of some ancient cargo cult, and sipped the semi-warm liquid. Had it been nectar of the gods, it would have been as ashes in our mouths.

But the last word goes to Baghdad (as in Baghdad — bombed all night).

'Well,' he said with a sigh. 'It certainly is a long way to Tipperary!'

A NEW EXPERIENCE
Barry McKiernan

My future brother-in-law, who had recently arrived from Holland, and I went to the local hotel for a drink. I bought the first round of drinks and future brother-in-law then went to the bar for his shout.

He came back a short time later with two beers and said (with a strong Dutch accent), 'What is this beer? There is Old beer and ...?'

I answered, 'New.'

He said, 'I wondered why the man laughed when I asked for two Young beers.'

A THIEF'S HOBBY
Bernard Skitt

The landlord of my local pub, Tom Collett MC, ex-RSM, Argyle and Sutherland Highlanders, was standing behind his lounge bar polishing glasses as he watched a lady customer surreptitiously sliding beer mats from the table into her handbag.

'Would Madam care to come to the bar? I will happily supply her with a complete selection of my beer mats rather than she clears them from the tables,' he called across the crowded bar.

The rather embarrassed lady made her way to the bar and stood before Tom, thanking him for being so kind.

'There must be a name for a collector of beer mats such as myself,' she said.

'There is, Madam,' Tom replied in a stern voice. 'A common bloody thief.'

AUNT BERTHA'S CURE
Marcia Carr

In the 1950s, my favourite relatives were Aunt Bertha and Uncle Bill. They were a happy couple, but Aunt Bertha was bothered by Uncle Bill's beer drinking.

Every weekend he would bring home a sugar bag of bottled beer and have a binge. But Bill was a fit man and a happy drunk, always cracking a joke and slipping me (a ten-year-old) two bob.

Then someone showed Aunt Bertha this ad.

She sent for this Eucrasy and when it arrived started putting it in his beer.

Like a lamb to the slaughter, he noticed no difference, but soon we all started to notice a difference in Uncle Bill. His hair started to fall out, he lost weight, he became morose. The doctors said he had stomach ulcers. Sadly, he died twelve months later.

People said, 'That's what the drink does to you,' but those of us in the know, knew it wasn't the beer but what was being put in it!

Heartbroken, lost, guilty — who knows? — Aunt Bertha died six months later.

I feel sorry for people who don't drink.

They wake up in the morning and that's the best they're going to feel all day.

Dean Martin

BALLARAT BERTIE
Ed Tonks

About sixteen years ago a friend returned from Ballarat with a couple of bottles of CUB's Ballarat Bitter featuring Ballarat Bertie on the label. By this stage I was becoming well known for my willingness to try different beers. After sampling a bottle with some workmates the question was asked, 'How do we obtain some of this stuff, short of going to Ballarat?'

Taking up the challenge I phoned the local CUB depot at Cardiff. The reply was negative at best. 'No market for that stuff here and you have no liquor licence so we can't get it for you. You'll have to order it from Ballarat yourself.'

Undaunted, I consulted the Ballarat phone book and jotted down a few numbers. Ballarat Cellars was the first I rang and it proved positive. 'No worries,' said the proprietor, 'I'll send you ten cases and I'll look after the transport this end.'

The beer duly arrived, the cost being shared by the number who were prepared to try the Ballarat drop.

Blokes being blokes, quite a number of bottles were shared by those who ordered it. The initial curiosity about this unfamiliar product was prompted by the Ballarat Bertie label, but the creamy smooth taste of the product produced more than a favourable reaction.

In about two months pressure mounted for another order, this time for twenty cases. Ballarat Cellars again delivered the goods.

In one quality control session the question was asked, 'How about ordering a pallet? How do you think that would go?'

I replied, 'No problem, as long as we have most of the money up front. By the way, how many cases in a pallet?'

I found out it was sixty-four.

I started to mobilise the order. With a firm commitment to fifty cases I ordered the pallet. Thus began a more serious association between my group and Ballarat Cellars which was to last for quite a number of years until CUB stopped making Ballarat Bitter.

I would like to think that our orders had an impact on CUB making Ballarat Bitter for as long as it did.

Shortly after the initial pallet order it was extended to two pallets which became the standard order, except for Christmas when we ordered three pallets.

The unloading of the beer truck was quite a social event. A group of blokes would converge on my house about twenty minutes before the scheduled arrival of the truck. It's amazing how quickly a job can be accomplished when the workers have a common motivation.

I can only guess at the number of people who obtained Ballarat Bitter as a result of my orders. As I mobilised the larger order each person in turn could mobilise their own order of five to ten cases.

As I mentioned, the Ballarat Bitter deliveries became a great social focus; they also gave a reason to keep in touch with former work colleagues and to broaden the network of friends.

For at least five people Ballarat Bitter was the only beer they purchased. Often the initiative for an order would come from members of the group itself and not from me.

Two pallets of Ballarat Bitter, 128 cases each containing one dozen long necks, carefully stacked and arranged in a suburban garage is an impressive sight, but alas, that is the past!

More recently a group of five people formed the Adamstown Heights Gentlemen's Club. It was formed at the suggestion of a friend and comprises three lower-middle-aged adult males and two young blokes in their early twenties.

The aims of the Gentlemen's Club are to enjoy each other's company whilst expanding one's knowledge of beer in order to appreciate the range of different tastes and styles.

At each meeting a member takes it in turn to invite a 'special guest' and tastings are held on a special themes basis. Themes to date include: Australia, Germany, United Kingdom, North America, Asia/Pacific, General Europe, Belgium ... Bertie, look what you started!

BANK INSPECTOR
Bill Jones

When a bank inspector called on a small country branch for a surprise audit he found the banking chamber deserted and the staff drinking beer in the manager's office. To teach them a lesson, he crept behind the counter and set off the hold-up alarm.

Much to his surprise, a barman from the pub next door immediately came running into the bank bearing a tray of fresh beers!

BANNED FROM THE WOODYARD
Peter Lalor

Harry M was your classic old-school publican. His mother was a publican, his wife was, his father-in-law was and by now his son, Spud, is probably following in the old man's footsteps.

You may have seen Harry; for a brief time back in the 1960s he was Australia's own Marlboro man. And so you'd have thought Harry would have had more sympathy for a thirsty horse.

One of the first family pubs Harry ran was Melbourne's Lord Newry (coincidentally, the Lord Newry in question was an equerry to the Queen or somebody like that) at the bottom of Brunswick Street in North Fitzroy.

It was a working-class suburb in those days and the Newry had an honest working-class clientele consisting of bank robbers, SP bookies, assorted ex-cons and the odd bloke who pulled a wage. Okay, maybe the latter outweighed the former but it was a colourful place, at least until the trendies moved in.

Anyway, it was a pretty busy pub, especially on a Saturday when Fitzroy (now the Brisbane Bears) were playing at home. The oval was about 100 metres from the pub and at half-time a desperate pack of footy fans would flock to the bar where 7oz glasses were filled at an astonishing rate by bar staff armed with the sheep-drench-type guns that were fitted to the end of a hose and allowed them to fill a glass anywhere within about two metres — or squirt anyone obnoxious within five.

One group of Harry's regulars were the guys from the woodyard on the other side of the footy ground.

These blokes could get a bit rowdy at times and occasionally a bit silly. One day the boss of the yard had the delivery horse out the front of the pub and decided he'd bring it in for a drink.

Despite earning a quid on the back of the Marlboro horse, Harry couldn't see the funny side of this and promptly barred the woodyard boss, who we'll call Joe.

Now, it can get pretty cold down in Melbourne

in winter and the pub of course got its wood from you know who.

When the first chill winds blew down Brunswick Street, Harry sent the barman down the road to buy some wood, but he came back empty-handed. Harry decided to go and see Joe who told him to f—k off out of his yard because he was barred.

For decades to come Harry would tell the yarn and boast that while he's met many a man who has been barred from a pub, he's never met another who was barred from a woodyard.

BEER AND MARRIAGE
Winston Lau

In 1995, I was living by myself and I saw a cooking program on television. They were making 'Fish and chips with a twist'. The 'twist' was adding a can of your favourite chilled beer to the batter. They also showed you how to make the side salad.

After watching the program and taking note of the recipe, I went to buy the ingredients at my local supermarket. I collected all the necessary ingredients and placed them on the check-out counter. I then noticed that the person in front of me had the same kind of ingredients: flour, eggs, vegetable oil, tomatoes, baby spinach, Spanish onions and a deli parcel wrapped in white paper. Surely it wasn't fish?

It was uncanny, bizarre, and it couldn't possibly have been the same recipe. That's what I was telling myself anyway, hoping that no one else would notice.

How embarrassing.

I had a quick glance at the lady in front of me and just smiled. I don't think she knew what was happening. I finally paid for my groceries and left the supermarket in a hurry.

I was still missing one ingredient — the beer — so I entered the local bottle shop, grabbed a can from the fridge and went to the counter.

Lo and behold, I saw the same lady with the same beer as was used on the television program. It was also the same as the one I had in my hand.

My suspicions were confirmed.

She was quite attractive and me being a bloke, I couldn't let the opportunity pass by. I started a conversation with her and found out that she also saw the TV program and yep, she was cooking for her parents that night.

Somehow I managed to ask her out and eight months later we got married. Every year since, we have celebrated our anniversary with 'Fish and chips with a twist'.

BEER AND SKITTLES
Chris Dwyer

I would like to pass on a story that makes me laugh whenever I rekindle thoughts of that silly Sunday years ago.

It was out in the central west of New South Wales and a few of us locals called into the Royal Hotel on a quiet Sunday afternoon. There were only about eight of us in the pub and we all settled back for a bit of a drink.

Later in the evening, with more than enough schooners aboard, a water cum beer fight erupted in the bar. The publican at the time, Frank W, couldn't keep out of a good fight so he hooked a hose to one of the beer lines and proceeded to spray down anyone who moved. Before you knew it we were sliding around in four inches of beer and water on the old lino floor.

The game we invented that day involved sliding along the length of the bar on your stomach with a bike helmet attached and hitting five 'skittles' with your head, the 'skittles' being two kegs placed on top of another three kegs.

Surprisingly, no one was hurt, but a few headaches were around the next day.

We found out later that Frank had to dispose of this lake of beer from his floor before his wife arose the next day.

We always thought Frank was a bit of a genius — he just drilled holes in the floor and drained the beer into the cellar.

BEER DRENCH
Penny Turner

A beer memory that springs to mind happened at one of our teenage parties held at home near Coonabarabran in the late 1960s. My father was a real wag as well as a good beer drinker, and was always thinking up tricks to play on us and our friends.

After an afternoon of playing tennis, eating and drinking, Dad appeared with a drench pack (a backpack normally filled with drench for sheep, cows, etc., that you squirted into the animal's mouth with a drench gun) on his back, full of beer. He proceeded to go around and drench our friends — if you wouldn't have the offered 'drench' orally, you ended up being squirted with beer.

Dad thought it was a huge joke, until the next morning when we got him with stale beer with the drench gun as he was waking up. Mum was not amused!

BLACK DAYS
Barry Williams

As a nipper (I was only sixteen) on the railways I used to go to the local pub — in fact the only pub — in the small town of Einasleigh in North Queensland with my two carpenter mates for a couple of beers while the camp oven stew was cooking. Our camp was only 200 yards out the back door of the pub by the railway siding.

On occasions there were Aboriginal stockmen or ringers out the back of the pub waiting for a ride back to the cattle station. This was back in the 1950s and publicans weren't allowed to sell beer or spirits to Aborigines, but some publicans would serve them drip tray beer — this was the stuff that spilt in the pour and was caught in the tray. The law soon cracked down on that and made sure the outback pubs put Condy's crystals in the drip tray and only sold beer in clear bottles. The rules were meant to put an end to the practice.

So this day Jimmy Carpentaria, an Aboriginal stockman from Carpentaria Station (they always took the name of the station as their surnames) asked me if I would bring out a bottle of 6d beer.

'Don't get the brown stuff,' he said. 'It tastes awful. Get me the purple beer. Better taste.'

BOGANS AND BEER
John Bogan

As you can see, my name is John Bogan. That's right, John BOGAN!

Growing up in the 1980s with this name was bad enough with the Kylie Mole skits in *The Comedy Company*. Now I hear 'bogan' has become an official word in the *Oxford English Dictionary*, defined as a 'depreciative term for an unfashionable, uncouth, or unsophisticated person, especially of low social status'.

Look, I am happy to cop the 'unfashionable' and maybe even the 'uncouth' in that definition, but when it comes to beer, my brother and I (no, his name isn't Dazza) would like to think we are fairly sophisticated. We travelled the US together tasting craft beers, and my own beer adventures since then have lead me to find a career in the craft brewing industry (no watery lagers for this bogan!).

So when we discovered a new craft beer from Tassie we wanted to try, I gave the brewery a call and left a message about having some sent to me. When they called me back, I could hear laughter in the background, like I was on speakerphone to the whole brewery, and the bloke talking to me was trying to stifle his own laugh while he asked for my name. Then, once I said my name, all he asked me was did I want a free shirt from the brewery.

Thinking these Tassie folk were a bit looney and starting to wonder if this beer they brewed even existed, it all made sense when he mentioned the brewery's slogan …

'Not suitable for bogans.'

… Safe to say, since then I have become an unofficial mascot for the brewery, and the beer we ordered from them is definitely suitable for these bogans!

BORN IN A PUB
Kevin Hole

The following is true as far as I have been informed; I personally cannot remember.

I was born on the 15th of April 1933 at the Mount Lachlan Hotel, corner of Elizabeth and Raglan Streets, Waterloo, Sydney.

Washed and clothed, my proud father, Jim, presented me to the local clientele from behind the bar.

As the tale goes, one inebriated gentleman promptly placed his forefinger in his glass of beer and then into my mouth.

Thus my first taste of beer, less than one hour old.

Furthermore, I still enjoy it!

CAR WENT THE OLD WAY HOME
Peter Lalor

There's an old Sunday newspaper editor who, like many in his trade, was fond of keeping the ink in his blood balanced with booze. Now Fozzie, as we'll call him, was prone to all-night sessions and tended to get rather muddled.

One night he headed home before sunrise and was obviously sober enough to find his car. (These were the days when that was proof enough of your ability to drive.)

Anyway, Fozzie got home safely enough, parked the car in the driveway, somehow made his way inside and upstairs to bed beside his dearly beloved and promptly began to snore away like he hadn't a trouble in the world.

At least, that's the way he tells it.

Early next morning he rolled over, almost killing his wife with his beery breath, opened one bloodshot eye and thought, 'Hang on a minute ... something's not right here.'

Poor Fozzie had woken up next to his first wife and somewhere in an adjacent suburb the second one was waiting in a very cranky mood.

'Bloody car went the old way home,' he told us later.

We believed him, but we're not sure if wife number two did.

COUNTING SHEEP
Chris Horneman

There's a story in our family about Dad not being able to sleep. He would lie there at night, tossing and turning. Mum suggested counting sheep, but that didn't work. In frustration she said, 'If you can't sleep and you can't count sheep try counting glasses of beer; that should come naturally to you.'

A few seconds passed and Dad got out of bed.

'Where are you going?' asked Mum.

'To get my first beer,' said Dad.

CROCKET
Peter Stehr

Crocket was the town character and regular at the Pioneer Hotel in the one-pub town of Boomi, northwest New South Wales.

It was noon on a November day in 1965 and a howling drought was in progress when a commercial traveller pulled up outside the hotel. He shook the dust off him and walked into the public bar where Crocket was sitting on a bar stool in the corner of the room.

The barmaid had just gone to the ladies room and the traveller waited impatiently for service, banging a two-shilling coin on the counter.

After a short while he turned to Crocket and said, 'How long has this town been dead for, mate?'

Crocket replied, 'Not long, mate; you're the first vulture to arrive.'

CURLY
Carole Smith

When I was a teenager in the 1960s, it was the 'in' thing to set our hair in rollers using beer as a setting agent. Amazingly, it worked. Our curls lasted all day.

Pity about the smell.

DRINK RIDER
Neil Chippendale

I belong to an organisation that recreates the battles of the English Civil Wars of 1642–1660. At one of the weekends in St Albans the founder of the organisation, the Brigadier, was riding his horse from pub to pub in full seventeenth-century battle gear and accepting drinks from members. After about two hours of this he was approached by the police and told to dismount, as he was drunk.

After about fifteen minutes he mounted up and rode off to the pubs again. A police car pulled up and the police arrested the 'Brig' and charged him with being drunk in charge of a horse. At court he was convicted and fined.

ERNIE
Peter Lalor

The Lord Newry regulars (see 'Banned from the Woodyard', p. 18) certainly had some history about them. One was an old bloke called Ernie, who by the time I got to know him looked like Billy McMahon's grandfather. Ernie was in his nineties and had big eyes and two enormous ears which must have continued to grow after the rest of him had started to shrink.

Ernie was so old he'd been a hansom cab driver in Brunswick Street as a lad.

Ernie loved a beer and would pop in most days as the Newry was early on his list of chores for the day.

Ernie was a busy man who knew almost everyone in Fitzroy and North Fitzroy and was always keen to catch up with every one of them at their individual pubs.

One day he was particularly downbeat when he dropped in for his first beer and told me that his best mate up at one of the other pubs had passed away, which left a bit of a hole in Ernie's routine. But, not for long.

When the bloke's will was read the relatives were horrified to find he had left an undisclosed sum in the care of the publican of his favourite pub and it was to be used to buy Ernie his beer every day.

Ernie was delighted and would check in each day and enjoy a shout from a dead mate.

FALSE TEETH
Garry Phipps

Old Mick had been drinking at his local pub for as long as anyone could remember and this day a young bloke came in and noticed that every time old Mick went to the toilet he would leave his false teeth in his beer.

Curiosity got the better of the young bloke so over he went and asked why.

Old Mick replied, 'I went to the toilet once and when I came back half me beer was missing, so in go the teeth and for some reason it doesn't happen any more.'

FLY IN BEER
Mrs E Shelley

In the good old days, around the early 1950s, I was living in Young, New South Wales. My late husband grew up in the area, but I had lived in Sydney all my life before moving there. We had two young children and not much money and I decided to earn a bit of extra cash one Sunday by cherry picking.

Leaving the two kids behind with a relative we set sail for the orchard which had advertised for cherry pickers. It was hard work for a city girl like me, but I was enjoying it.

About 10 a.m. the orchard owner's wife came out with freshly made scones and cakes and large pots of tea for our morning tea break.

One old-timer, a typical Aussie, got his tea and a fly fell into it.

'I'll have to throw that one out,' he said. 'You never know what germs they carry.'

Later that afternoon the same kind lady came out with some beer for all who wanted it and you would not believe it — the same old-timer got his beer, put it on the bench for a minute and a fly fell into it.

He got it out with his dirty finger and said, 'You can't waste a good beer,' and promptly drank it.

This is a true story and I've never been able to work out how he could not drink his tea, but the beer was okay.

HEAD BANGER
Paul Cairns

I was enjoying my second pint of Canberra Pride with the then Master Brewer for the Wig & Pen pub, Richard Pass. Richard was explaining the palate qualities of a higher temperature, slightly hopped, slightly malty ale and, being dedicated to the enjoyment of all things brown, dark brown and black, I was into it.

In keeping with this tour and with my palate being challenged at every mouthful, Richard suggested a change to an effervescent cold Kiandra Gold.

This was really hitting the spot, and two of these — followed by explanations and tasting of the wonderful Ballyragget Red — had me slightly infected but raring to go.

Richard's next choice, the intriguingly named but superb tasting Aviator Bock, had me asking for detailed recipes and further explanation regarding its naming. I must confess that by now Richard was slightly infected himself.

With some mirth he announced the following: 'Bock is a high alcohol content dark beer enjoyed by German landowners and the like and one should look out for one's self when consuming more than the one or two. In fact, true to its name, "Bock" is the last thing you will hear as your head hits the tiles on the pub floor!'

So endeth the tour and the lesson.

You're not drunk if you can lie on the floor without holding on.

Joe E Lewis

HORSE-PITELL-ITY
Lloyd O'Brien

Many years ago on the kind of stinking hot evening that only Sydney can turn on, I took a visiting Scottish friend down to the Quay for a ferry ride.

Sydney left him speechless.

'What,' I asked cockily, 'is it that you particularly like about our city?'

'Och aye, it's yer horse-pitell-ity, no doubt abert-it.'

We had moved to a seat close to the berthing ferry when I noticed someone had left a brown paper bag there. In it were two very cold, very large bottles of beer.

'Yes,' I said, not missing a beat and reaching for the trusty bottle opener I carried back then. 'It even extends to this arrangement for leaving a couple of coldies around the traps for parched blow-ins from Scotland.'

Glug-glug-glug ... we each took a few healthy swigs.

I smiled at him confidentially. 'You're lucky, you know, mate; you're drinking a Reschs Dirty Annie.'

He frowned a little, then quickly put the bottle to his mouth and drained it.

'Aye, it's yer horse-pitell-ity!' was all he could say.

HOW'S ABOUT A KISS?
James Hamilton

As an avid armchair gardener, his nose attracted me at once. In my time I have judged Italian tomatoes and early lettuce and was once co-opted onto a sub-committee to discuss the merits of a particularly fine King Edward potato. His nose, had it been in a different position, could well have won a prize in the red onion section of the local horticultural show.

After that, the rest of his face was something of a disappointment. There were hints of glorious purple in the broken veins that littered his cheeks like motorway intersections and the puce of his ears matched a popular shade of lipstick in an economy range. But the foundation was a common, agricultural ruddiness that can only have come from life out-of-doors.

I rather pride myself on my complexion. I inherited it from my mother. When she died at eighty-three after a blameless life led entirely without recourse to artificial face creams, the undertaker in an undertone remarked that she had one of the finest skins he had seen during forty years in the trade.

Recollected gems like that can enrich many a winter morning. I admit that I do use 'Bliss' just to keep the wrinkles at bay; I believe I owe it to my friends. Of course, one's diet is so important, too. Rich foods I avoid like the plague and alcohol I take only in moderation.

However, that particular evening was an exception. I really could have killed for a glass of beer. I had just spent a frightful four hours driving in pouring rain on an outback track that more closely resembled the Limpopo River mudflats than a vehicular thoroughfare. Only the absence of hippopotami persuaded me that I was still in Australia.

I found the hotel quite by chance; in the gathering dusk its welcoming lights presaged a life-saving oasis. It stood in splendid isolation as a memorial to a short-lived copper-mining boom in the 1890s and it was clear that precious little had been spent on it since.

A Trappist monk would have felt at home in my cell-like bedroom, while anyone lucky enough to find the bathroom could have been inspired to write a treatise on the history of plumbing. I moved closer to the bar with the hesitant anticipation of an occasional drinker trespassing on private ground.

He was the only occupant of the Public Bar. He squinted at me from beneath bushy eyebrows that sprouted haphazardly like the whiskers of a mature walrus. His greasy, greying hair receded from a furrowed forehead and cascaded untidily into a ponytail.

The fragrance of his pomade was intriguing and not one with which I was familiar; a member of the Salvation Army might have recognised it. I use 'Sensation'; in an instant it suggests masculinity without the obtrusive biceps, and culture without an overtly gay label. I have also found that a little 'Power' on the cheeks after shaving encourages women to be more attentive. It hints at hidden wealth without fostering undue extravagance.

His clothing was what I would describe as bush or weekend Australian. He wore a tee shirt that stretched optimistically but not entirely successfully over a sagging stomach. It clearly had only a nodding acquaintance with the laundrette and I could not possibly repeat its illustrated caption in mixed company.

The pungency of his sun-dried sweat reminded me of Moroccan camel dung; not entirely unpleasant in the thin night air at a Berber encampment on the edge of the Sahara Desert but somewhat overpowering within the confines of a Public Bar. The leather belt supporting his jeans was only narrowly winning the battle of decency. His muddy sneakers added to the unwashed aura that surrounded him.

Although sartorial elegance is not a noticeable feature of the Australian outback, I believe my outfit on that occasion would have found favour with my tailor. After a long bath liberally dosed with essential oils, I chose neutral colours. My silk tie, reminiscent of ripening corn, accompanied a cream shirt and a fetching sleeveless pullover in Nile Sand that my Aunt Edith had given me at my request the Christmas before. My cotton trousers were Inca Stone, a popular choice in London that year, while pale tangerine socks contrasted rather well with shoes in a nice shade of African native brown. (There, I have remembered not to use that other word.)

He said nothing, but gazed pensively into his empty glass as I approached the bar. I detected stale tobacco smoke and instinctively looked for his nicotine-stained fingers and matching teeth to confirm his addiction to the weed.

I am not an intolerant man but I do dislike tobacco smoke. It assaults my senses and permeates my clothing; it lingers like a malevolent spirit, abroad long after it should have been laid to rest. I sniffed the air sensitively in much the same way that a prairie dog assesses imminent danger in the Arizona desert; against all odds, my craving for beer kept me moving forward.

As I stood at the bar I inclined my head towards him. Experience has taught me that presenting a friendly disposition to the natives does no harm, however unsavoury strange bars may be. However, in my opinion, too much familiarity breeds contempt and should be avoided at all costs.

I believe that an Englishman's self-sufficiency in foreign lands can be traced back to the Norman Conquest and the conquerors' penchant for constructing castles; I plan to write a monograph on the subject on my return to England.

He did not return my glance at first. In the light of subsequent events, he may have been shy or perhaps just suffering from the early stages of dipsomania. A slight twitch of the hand holding his empty glass did suggest that drink was uppermost in his mind.

The first words he uttered were indistinct. They sounded like 'Pommy bastard'. He might have said 'Tommy Custard', although that's not my name.

Perhaps Tommy was the barman.

The next words were clearer. 'Have a beer, mate.' My moment had arrived. I beamed at him in a manner calculated to put him at his ease. 'That's very kind of you,' I said as I sat down on a bar stool beside him. 'I'll have a Four Kisses please.'

I think he misunderstood me. With an agility that surprised me and would probably have alarmed his doctor, he reached the exit in ten seconds flat.

As the door swung shut, his parting words echoed like thunder across the bar. 'Pommy bastard' was clearer this time but I was unable to recognise everything that followed.

The barman later told me that he had never before heard such a fine range of Australian expletives expressed in such a short space of time. I consider myself fortunate to have been present.

HUMPTY DUMMIES
Paul Staunton

While I was travelling around Australia with a mate we stumbled across a pub in Humpty Doo in the Northern Territory. With the locals just being their bizarre selves, we decided to sit for a while.

We got talking and drinking cold ales from the tap after a great but stinking hot day, when the locals told us that the fishing club was having a do on that night.

We stayed, but at the end of the night had to drive two kilometres to a camping spot for the night. There was a policeman outside the pub waiting for the first person to take off for home as everyone in the pub was drunk (and driving).

One person in the pub was not drinking so I suggested that he walk outside, pretend to stumble to his car, and drive off very quickly in the opposite direction to which most of us were going.

He took off in his car. The policeman gave chase and everybody piled out into their cars and straight home. Everyone got home alive, well, and without coming across the constabulary.

One of the funniest sights was watching all the people run for their cars as if there was a breakout at the prison.

We called back the next day and they were still laughing; I think they were still drunk too.

I SAW THE LIGHT
Bruce Dowling

One Friday night in 1983 I'd had a long session at the Drummoyne Rowing Club. Then one of my mates asked me if I wanted to go with them to Vaucluse. I figured they were going to a party so I said yes.

There were four of us in the car, but one bailed at Double Bay because the driver was a maniac.

When we got to Vaucluse my mate (no names) in the front of the car got out and I figured he was just checking out how the party was. After a while I asked the driver why he was taking so long and his answer led me to believe that the guy was doing a break and enter.

Now, I wasn't so keen to hang around, but in my condition I wasn't able to go too far. It was a very windy night and with all the beer I'd drunk I soon needed to go for a piss. The only place I could see that would give me shelter was a house under construction down the street at a T intersection.

After I'd had a leak I stepped up from the clay in the front of the yard and saw searchlights in the sky and straight away thought that the police helicopter had been called in to search for my mate.

I couldn't hear the helicopter because there was a gale blowing, but it was hanging around so I went back to the house and waited. I kept checking, but the helicopter was still there and I was too scared to go back to the car in case I was seen.

Next thing I knew I woke up with floorboards inches from my face ... I'd fallen asleep under the house. It's amazing where you can sleep after a few beers. Anyway, I climbed out from under the house, covered in clay and trying to remember what had happened the previous night.

As I stepped up onto the footpath and lit a cigarette it all started to come back. Then I looked up to where I'd seen the helicopter, feeling relieved I hadn't been caught up in the mess, only to find I was looking at the South Head lighthouse!

IT AIN'T HEAVY ...
Martin New

My wife and I were recently invited to my sister's home for Christmas dinner.

My brother-in-law Len is a keen beer lover and for Christmas we had bought him a 24-bottle case of 'Celebrate the Millennium' Crown Lager.

I had planned to drive from our home on the Central Coast to Lorraine and Len's place at Jannali, but my wife, knowing that I like a celebratory drink myself, insisted we travel by train for safety.

I had to lug the heavy case of beer over two kilometres to our nearest railway station, sit it on my lap for safekeeping on the one and a half hour journey to Central Station, carry it again for what seemed like miles to the train platform for services to Jannali, and hold on to it for the forty-minute journey to Jannali and then walk from the station, finishing with the climb up a steep hill to our destination.

To ease the burden I sang a song on the way: 'It ain't heavy (well, it was, but you know what I mean), it's for my brother.'

I was so relieved when I touched down at my sister's, and just found enough strength to grab my first coldie for Chrissie.

Len was overjoyed with this thoughtful gift, which made the effort worth the while.

Imagine my surprise upon opening my Christmas present from Lorraine and Len to find — you guessed it — a 24-bottle case of 'Celebrate the Millennium' Crown Lager.

Of course, I took it home with me on our long return journey. There was no way I was going to leave 'my' carton with beer-loving Len.

The problem with some people is that when they aren't drunk, they're sober.

William Butler Yeats

MEDICINAL PURPOSES
Glenn Gilbert

In the late 1980s my family owned a small holiday home on the northern Central Coast of New South Wales. Situated in an ideal location close to the beach, lake and local watering hole, it was the venue for many memorable weekends shared amongst a large circle of friends aged in their mid-twenties. We would regularly travel from our homes in northern Sydney on a Friday evening to spend our leisure hours surfing, fishing and of course partaking of the odd ale.

As one particular weekend approached the usual sojourn was planned. On the Thursday before, I was approached by a friend named Mark who was overjoyed at having a half work day on Friday; he asked if he could have the house keys to travel up early with another friend to get a head start on the weekend. Mark was a trusted friend; therefore I could see no reason to deny this request.

Arrangements were made for him to pick up the keys from our house at lunchtime on Friday.

The following day Mark arrived on time, perched upon his preferred mode of transport — the beloved Suzuki 750cc motorcycle. Surprisingly, another friend, Chris, who at the time was unemployed, had made a spur of the moment decision to travel with Mark as a pillion passenger. They were leaving early to enjoy the fine weather, and spent a short time with my mother before heading off with sleeping bags and luggage attached to the rear of the cycle.

I arrived home around 3 p.m., and within an hour was joined by the others who intended travelling that afternoon. Just prior to our departure I received a phone call from Chris. They had come off Mark's motorcycle on the F3 Freeway, and he had been transported to Hornsby Hospital by ambulance with some minor leg injuries. Mark's whereabouts were unaccounted for; however, Chris assured me he was not badly injured. Despite our concerns, Chris assured us he was okay and would soon be discharged into his mother's care (she was already there).

I made a few phone calls, but in those days before the mobile phone if someone wasn't home it was anyone's guess as to what they were up to. I did establish, however, that Mark was not taken to hospital. So with that unexpected delay we commenced the hour-long journey north.

On the way the conversation centred on Mark. What had happened? How was he? Where was he? We need not have worried, for our minds were soon to be put at ease. As we neared the holiday house I saw the blinds were parted and the wooden front door clearly open behind the mesh door. Our convoy of vehicles stopped out the front and the group slowly congregated outside the front door. Someone was certainly home. Most of us assumed that Mark had somehow managed to continue his journey.

However, several hard knocks on the door failed to draw any response. We circled round the back through the old steel gate and as the rear yard came into view I saw a sight I will never forget.

Mark had managed to ride his somewhat worse for wear motorcycle to the house and park it in the rear yard. He had then grabbed a full carton of cold beer stubbies and a beanbag from the house. He had placed the beanbag in the middle of the back yard, cut the bottom out of the beer carton, exposing the base of the stubby bottles, then placed the carton upside down in the bean bag. He had then positioned his red raw rump, complete with gravel rash and lacerations, squarely in the centre of the beer in an attempt to alleviate the pain of the road rash he suffered in the accident. His shredded and bloody jeans were draped across the crashed motorcycle.

So there he was, sunning himself in the middle of the yard with his bum on a slab. He looked at us and said, 'See, guys, I told you the beer is strictly for medicinal purposes.'

The rest of the weekend was just as interesting, but this memory is priceless and permanently etched in my mind.

MY UNCLE
Terry Hayes

My favourite beer story concerns my cousin's wedding, which occurred in April 1955 when bottled beer was very scarce.

Having frequented the local pub for the major part of his working life, my uncle was able to talk the publican into parting with a few bottles of the precious liquid.

The future groom, with the help of his intended father-in-law, ended up with ten dozen large bottles which they stored under the uncle's bed. A very safe place to keep it, for the wedding was only two weeks away.

Although not yet retired from work, my uncle took a few days off to get things ready for the wedding.

The beer was purchased on Tuesday; the following Monday my uncle came out in the morning complaining of being a bit crook. 'And rightly so,' said his daughter. 'You should be dead, you bastard; you've drunk all the grog.'

Upon investigation the ten dozen were ten dozen empty bottles as well as three whisky, one brandy and one Pimms bottle. Fair enough, a good drink for a little under a week; however, he still managed to carry out his regular sessions at the local every day.

The same uncle came home after a big session with his mate and realised he had no keys to get inside. After a lot of discussion, they decided to get in through the laundry window. Using a ladder from under the house, and after much difficulty, the window was opened and uncle slid in, into a tub full of soaking washing. Naturally, when they came to open the door they found that it had not been locked.

My uncle's drinking bouts are a legend in an unbelievable family history.

OUCH
Louise Carr

We were holidaying on the Central Coast several years ago. Dad was planning a big Australia Day party and had been buying stacks of beer which was all stored in an old fridge on the verandah of the two-storey house where we were staying.

Mum and Dad were staying overnight in Sydney and my sister and I were alone in this strange house. We heard a car pull up nearby and, spying through the blinds, we saw two youths heading for the house, apparently up to no good.

Downstairs was well locked but upstairs the verandah area was quite open. To our horror one of them started to climb the tall timber pole leading to the verandah.

'They're after Dad's beer,' we whispered.

'Never!' we agreed.

I told my sister to ring 000 and to ring Dad while I grabbed some cold tinnies and started throwing them at the invader. I'm a netball player and I didn't miss with many.

The climber was taking a battering but still seemed to be coming up.

We knew the police were a long way away and would take ages to get there and the other thief had started to climb up the other pole.

We were just about to give up the attack and retreat to the bedroom, which had sturdy locks, when we heard a siren. No, not the police, it was an ambulance coming to the would-be thieves' rescue.

Apparently, in her panic my sister had been giving the operator a blow by blow description. 'Ooh! She's hit him on the head ... Ooh! She's hit him again!'

The woman thought the intruders needed an ambulance more than we needed the police.

Fortunately the siren's noise was enough to scare the robbers and they took off.

We saved Dad's beer.

Dad said we deserved a medal, but we settled for a trip to Surfers.

Oh, the party was a great success and probably resulted in a few more sore heads.

PRAISE GOD AND PASS THE VB
David Keane

Here is my favourite beer story. It sounds like a tall tale, but I can assure you that every word is true, because it happened to me.

I had just come out from a church meeting and was attempting to start my car. No matter how hard I tried, I could not get the engine to come to life.

It seemed that it was out of petrol, so my pastor took me for a ride to the petrol station to fill up a tin. We came back and emptied the tin of fuel in the petrol tank and tried again, but still nothing.

By now we had three pastors and some friends surrounding the car.

Two friends of one of the men present were walking along the road, after having consumed several longnecks of VB. Each was carrying a bottle as they walked. They approached us and watched for a couple of minutes while we poured some petrol in the carburettor and tried to start the engine, still without luck. (It turned out later that the fuel line was blocked.)

Soon one of these two piped up and said that he had a solution. He downed the rest of his beer and poured some petrol into the bottle. He instructed me to keep turning the key and pressing the accelerator, while he continued to pour petrol from his bottle into the carburettor.

This seemed to give it some life for a few seconds, and then suddenly I saw a huge flash from where I sat in the car. The petrol had caught alight and this bloke was holding a 'Molotov cocktail'.

To make things worse, the engine bay had caught alight as the petrol spilt out of the bottle.

It was like an inferno. What happened next occurred over a couple of seconds, but it seemed like an eternity.

The spectators by now had moved a couple of metres away onto a driveway. This bloke with the blazing VB looked at the bottle, looked at me and looked back at the bottle. His eyes went wide and he lobbed the bottle up into the air, and bang, straight onto the driveway in the middle of the onlookers.

The driveway went up in flames while people went diving for cover. (No one was burnt, thank the Lord.)

Meanwhile, I was sitting in the driver's seat watching my engine bay go up in flames.

Quick as a flash, the other bloke ripped the twist top off his unopened longneck and proceeded to shake it vigorously. He then sprayed the golden drop into the engine bay and put the fire out. I couldn't believe it.

I know that if we'd had a video camera we would have won 'Australia's Funniest Home Videos' with this effort. One thing is for sure — I don't think I will ever again hear three pastors and a group of Christians declaring the virtues of VB so enthusiastically!!

Reality is an illusion that occurs due to lack of alcohol.

Anonymous

SCHOONER GRIP
Garry Phipps

A mate of mine once did a favour for a friend. When the job was finished the friend asked, 'How much do I owe you?'

'Don't worry about it; buy me a beer next time you're in the pub,' my mate replied.

A couple of weeks later the friend walked into the local, saw my mate and ordered an extra beer. He walked over to him and said, 'Here's that beer I owe you,' and handed it to him.

It promptly fell through my mate's outstretched hand and smashed on the pub floor.

'Why did you drop that beer?' the bloke asked.

'Because,' my mate replied patiently, 'this is a Schooner Grip not a Middy Grip.'

Needless to say he was bought schooners from then on and they fitted perfectly.

SINKING A BEER
Norm Woodcock

This story goes back to the year 1935 when I was prospecting at a place called Southern Cross in the Western Australian goldfields.

Two old prospectors sank a shaft in the main street of the town, opposite the hotel, and spent as much time in the pub as working in the mine.

As the shaft got deeper the bloke operating the windlass would pop into the pub, come out with two foaming pots of beer and call out to his mate at the bottom of the shaft that 'a beer was coming down'. He would put a pot on top of the bucket attached to the cable of the windlass and ever so carefully lower the beer to his mate.

This procedure was repeated many times throughout the day.

I had the privilege of sharing a couple of beers with them on a few occasions and learned a lot from their experiences as prospectors and Drinkers of Beer.

THAT COCKY'S DEAD
Norm Woodcock

During the 1930s I met up with a couple of old prospectors in a pub at a place called Marvel Loch on the goldfields of Western Australia. After a few beers they told me they were about to have a few tons of gold-bearing quartz transported to the Government Battery for crushing.

To save them a few bob I offered to cart the ore in my T Model Ford (converted to a utility truck) to the Battery. The crushing yielded about 20oz of nugget gold worth about 100 quid.

These two old boys were very thankful for my help and insisted on repaying me, so off we went to a place called Southern Cross and booked into a boarding house for the night.

Next stop: the local pub for a 'few' beers.

Like all prospectors, these two guys could put away the beer. After a while I left them to it, went to the boarding house and had a feed, then went upstairs to an open verandah which contained three beds, one cage and one cockatoo.

My two friends returned several hours after, their arms laden with bottles of beer. They were up and down all night, drinking and urinating in the cocky's cage. The poor cocky would splutter and squawk every time they went to the cage, which was quite understandable.

And so it went on, until suddenly there was a squawk and an eerie silence.

I managed a little sleep but was up at dawn to see my two companions dead to the world. I looked in the cage and saw the poor bloody bird — stone dead on the bottom of the cage.

I still don't know to this day whether the cocky died of poisoning, drowning or a screwed neck — probably all three, I fancy.

I had those two blokes out of bed and into Tin Lizzie and off to Marvel Loch before they were awake.

I took sympathy on the old prospectors and dropped into a pub on the way back. Needless to say, I gave that boarding house a wide berth whenever in Southern Cross.

I met many prospectors on the goldfields and they were a great bunch of fellows. These two were no exception and I guess they are still prospecting up in the Great Beyond. I hope Saint Peter shouts them a beer now and then — and doesn't let them anywhere near the cockies.

THE LOST BEERS
Paulene Lowe

Many years ago my husband was organising a barbecue during the war years. He and his mates would buy schooners of beer and fill quart bottles, as take-away beer was as rare as hen's teeth.

They were going to Sans Souci near Mick Moylan's Hotel to have a barbecue on the beach.

My husband said he would keep the beer cold by burying it in the sand near the surf. After a while everything was ready so he went to get the beer, but couldn't find it as the tide had come in.

He had to outrun all his mates and hitch home.

THERE IS A GOD
Mark Bressington

This is a true story. I went to a Catholic high school in the Manly Warringah area (St Augustine's College in Brookvale). When I was in Year Twelve, I had an Irish priest, Father Ward, a teacher of Religious Education.

As we were in our final year of school the class was fairly relaxed and Father Ward treated us with the respect that young adults deserve. I remember that during one of the classes someone asked Father Ward if he really believed in God and miracles.

We were fortunate enough to have the following story told to us as his way of replying to the question.

It was the middle of summer on a Sunday, one of those days when the temperature rose over forty degrees early in the afternoon. Father Ward had performed a Mass earlier that day and was trying to enjoy the rest of his Sunday as God had intended — putting his feet up and watching the cricket on the TV.

The heat was becoming unbearable and as the majority of ads on the TV between overs were beer commercials, he started to long for an ice cold beer. As a priest, he was on a weekly allowance of about $7 a week and as a smoker, he had already blown his allowance and did not have the money to nip down the road to the pub to buy a beer.

He looked to the heavens and prayed for a beer. A little while later there was a knock on the door. Father Ward arose from a heat-induced coma to see who it was. When he opened the door there was no one to be seen.

He looked down, and there sitting on the step was a six-pack of ice cold beer with a note attached.

He bent down and picked up the beer and read the note.

It was from a parishioner who had been in Mass that morning. The parishioner wanted to thank Father Ward for his moving sermon which had been a comfort to him and, it being such a hot day, he felt a cold beer was the best way of doing so.

Now, the priest's not sure if God had heard his plea for a beer, or if God had told the parishioner to deliver the beer, or if it was God who had inspired his sermon in Mass that morning. One thing he was sure of — he was thankful to God for the ice cold beer.

THIS ONE LOOKS ARMLESS
Peter Lalor

Like most Australian blokes Gordon L was prepared to go the extra yard for the institutions he held dearest. Now we're not talking surf clubs, scout groups or even local government. Gordon, like many of us, loved his local and would do anything for the boys and their home away from home.

After one heavy session Gordon and a mate were driving along a road about 100 kilometres south of Darwin when they saw a snake. It was clearly too early to have the DTs so the lads knew this crawling creepy was the real thing.

Remembering that the boys back at the pub dearly wanted a python for the fish tank — don't even ask what happened to the fish — Gordon decided to take matters in hand.

He stumbled out onto the road and with his best beer goggles on attempted to grab what was clearly a harmless boa constrictor.

Course it ish!

Well, almost harmless and almost a python; unfortunately, Gordon had set his muddled sights on a 2.8-metre deadly king brown snake with a head the size of a fist.

'I made the mistake of grabbing it with my left hand because I was holding a beer in my right,' he said later.

You can see from our intrepid bushman's comments that he was perhaps a little more devoted to his beer than his health and things were clearly going to get a little sticky.

'I had its head in my hand, but it got loose and grabbed the web of my left hand. Its fangs were that big it ripped my hand open,' Gordon said.

Still gripping the beer, he wrestled the snake into a sack, never spilling a drop in the process.

Gordon, like most of us who've woken with a hangover only to go back and fight the good fight next Friday night, was not a man who was once bitten twice shy. Angry, confused, and perhaps not thinking as clearly as he should have, he stuck his hand back in the bag.

Maybe he was making sure it really was a biting snake.

'I stuck my hand back in the bag and it must have smelled blood,' Gordon said. 'It bit me another eight times.'

Upset by the snake's hostility, Gordon withdrew and started to lose consciousness, but luckily for him he had a friend who cared.

'My mate was trying to keep me awake by whacking me in the head and pouring beer on me,' Gordon recalls.

His good friend decided to drive him to Darwin, but only got as far as the Noonamah Hotel, about fifty kilometres from the city, where the bar manager called an ambulance.

Sensible bloke that.

Gordon was in a coma for six weeks and had continuous blood transfusions because the venom prevented clotting and caused internal bleeding.

Up at the Darwin hospital they don't muck around and they decided to lop off the poor bloke's arm. His heart stopped three times during the amputation — probably shocked that it would be going through life with one less drinking apparatus.

The doctors said that Gordon was the sickest man ever to survive a snake bite, although you probably didn't need a medical degree to figure that out.

'I still can't believe my arm's been chopped off,' Gordon said later.

Gordon's sister reckoned her brother was accident-prone.

'He's like a cat, but this time he has used up his ninth life,' she said.

Gordon once spent three months in hospital after his car hit a buffalo and was crushed when a truck reversed and pinned him to a pile of bricks.

'I still have my life and I guess that's the most important thing,' Gordon said later.

Yeah, pal, but what about the bloody boys at the pub? What about the fish tank? Talk about self-centred!

WATER CLOSET
Peter Lalor

Back where I came from, a particular local businessman and his family were held in pretty high esteem. They were a nice enough family, but some of the older boys didn't quite live up to the high standards set by their mother and father.

One night the lads played up when the olds were out and got a little carried away. When the parents got home they noticed nothing wrong until they got out of the car and heard groaning from the garden bed by the driveway.

Dad got the torch and steering lock and approached the noise with some caution. Moving the torch around the ferns and what have you he couldn't help but notice a smell and then, to his horror, he found a near-naked man semi-conscious among the plants.

After some further investigation it was established that this rather drunk and bruised person was the number two son who had fallen from the balcony above while taking a leak.

Worse was in store.

The mother opened the door of the house to hear terrible cries from the bedroom of number three son, the youngest. Running in, she was passed by son number one who appeared to be sleepwalking in his underpants.

Inside number three's room was a terrible scene.

The sobbing little fella told Mum how his big brother had come barging in and without a word had opened the wardrobe, pulled out the sock drawer, urinated in it, pushed the drawer back in, closed the door and then left.

It seems the eldest had turned left instead of right and in his rather inebriated state had mistaken the kid's closet for a water closet.

Apparently this isn't an unusual thing, as I knew a bloke who mistook his turntable (remember them?) for the urinal. He'd wandered into the lounge room, lifted the lid and closed it again when finished — clearly a bloke under the thumb.

WATER POLICE, WARM FEET AND A BEER SHOWER
R T Noble

Back in the late 1950s I used to drink in a pub in Penshurst Street, Chatswood, called Ryans. Pretty tough pub too; bloodhouse they used to call it.

In this pub drank a bloke called Old Sepp — great old bloke sober, but after three pints he thought he was superman.

Anyway, poor Old Sepp was always getting turfed out, usually spending the night in the local lockup.

This particular night he saw the police coming and took off out the door and jumped into the old horse trough that was still there and yelled, 'You can't touch me. This is a job for the water police.'

In those days — late 1950s, early 1960s — you could not get a drink on a Sunday unless you went to Windsor or Penrith (bonafide traveller, it was called).

Anyway, we used to have barbecues nearly every Saturday night ending late Sunday. One night all thirty of us flaked out round the large fire we had.

Next morning a mate called Monty woke up groaning, 'Geez, my feet.' He went to stand up and fell over. We rushed over to help him and when we removed his boots the bottoms of his feet fell off. It seems his feet had cooked through his boots as he was too near the fire. The poor bugger was in hospital for weeks and off work for months.

When we asked him what woke him up, he said, 'I got cold.'

Monty, the same bloke, was always tinkering with home-brew. The only trouble was, he could not stick to his recipe.

I remember one brew he put down; some clown told him to add raisins to it to give it a kick. He invited a half dozen of his mates to try it out. Bloody hell! Talk about dynamite! Bloody bottles blew up everywhere. Blokes had cut hands, cut faces — beer all over us.

When we finally got a few poured it tasted like Purple Para (the cheap plonk of the day) with a head on it. The bloody stuff was so dangerous we had to throw a blanket over the remaining bottles and were not game to go near it. I think Monty ended up throwing rocks at them to smash the damn things.

WATERING DOWN THE BEER
Hillary Greenup

It was Christmas day 2000 in Ballina and we were very much anticipating the scrumptious lunch ahead of us. The day was hot and humid and what better way to start out than to have a nice cold drink? For my mum and myself it was a glass of champers, for the boys a cold beer — Cane Toad beer, in fact! It came as part of a Christmas food hamper sent by my brother. From memory, the Cane Toad beer packed a punch at 7 per cent alcohol content.

In view of this fact, my dad, not being too much of a seasoned drinker, like my husband, Steve, decided to make his into a shandy. Steve had made a special trip down to the local shop to grab a bottle of lemonade. So Dad proceeded to dilute his Cane Toad beer with the lemonade.

Each time he took a swig he couldn't believe just 'how strong this bloody Cane Toad beer is', so much so that he went back to the fridge to get that bottle of lemonade about three times! What he really couldn't understand was why the beer wasn't getting a nice head — the more lemonade he added, the flatter it went. He thought that the strength of the alcohol must be causing the lemonade to go instantly flat!

It wasn't until Steve noticed that the bottle of lemonade he had bought hadn't yet been opened, that the 'penny dropped'. Dad had been using the bottle of cold water (incidentally, in a lemonade bottle) to 'water' his beer down! In the end a glass of champagne was in order while Steve enjoyed his full strength Cane Toad beer! On our return to Sydney, my brother asked how Dad had enjoyed the beer ... Well, um ...

A tavern is a place where madness is sold by the bottle.

Jonathan Swift

WATERING THE GARDEN
Mary Smith

After a long night of good friends, good food and good beer, hubby, after saying his farewells as they drove away, 'took short'. As the little house was already occupied, he decided to water the flowers beneath the small rail-less balcony. He took one step too many, breaking his leg on the concrete surround.

On arrival, the ambulance officers asked how he fell. He promptly told them he had been pushed.

'Pushed by whom?' they asked.

'Hahn,' was the reply.

'Hahn who?' asked the ambulance officer.

'Hahn Ice,' he replied.

After a pin and plate inserted and six weeks in plaster I guess he'll watch where he waters next time (or how much he drinks).

WRONG NUMBER
June Benson

It was a much more innocent time. Christmas Eve, about 5 p.m., temperature hovering around 100 degrees. My mother, a devout and unquestioning Catholic, sat fanning herself on the front verandah.

The sound of our phone intruded on the heavy atmosphere.

'It's yerself, Mrs Shepherd?'

My mother recognised Father O'Dougherty's voice.

'Would yer be so good as ter send me around a half dozen of the usual cold ones as soon as yer can?'

My mother, although none too pleased, agreed.

'I think he drinks Sheaf Stout,' she said crossly, pulling me by one ear as I attempted to beat a hasty retreat, and reaching for her purse.

Soon I was staggering to the presbytery door.

'What's this lovely beer you've got here, Junie Benson?'

Father O'Dougherty was completely puzzled.

It turned out he thought he'd rung Shepherd's corner store for his weekly supply of Marchant's lemonade.

However, he did NOT insist I take the Sheaf Stout home and I've always believed it did not go to waste.

FROTHY FACTS

A SAD END

The story about the man drowning in a vat of beer at the brewery has made its way into folklore. However, there may just be some truth to it.

In the 1890s a brewer named Joseph Hartley was found floating in a tank of beer at the Castlemaine brewery in Victoria. He was dead, although it is not known if he had fought off any attempts to save him.

The customs officers and health authorities insisted the beer be run off down the street gutters and a broken-hearted group of spectators gathered to watch.

One paper at the time suggested that Hartley had become 'too much absorbed in his business'.

The Bulletin magazine published a poem at the time, bemoaning the loss of the beer and Hartley. In part, it read:

For poor old Joseph Hartley,
The poet sighs, or partly,
And likewise drops a tear.
But not for Joseph only,
In the graveyard lying lonely.
Doth the poet drop a tear,
So crystal, bright and clear
He is thinking, thinking, thinking,
Of that liquor brewed for drinking.

BARMAID BANS AND THE BEER UPRISING

Did you know that until 1967 barmaids were banned in South Australia? Most other states had hosted anti-barmaid campaigns, and while they were not successful in New South Wales (in 1884 a bill was defeated by just one vote) or Western Australia, they were in South Australia and Victoria.

In Victoria 346 licences were issued in 1885 to barmaids as a means of ending the pernicious practice of allowing women to serve beer. The licensed girls were to be the last of their kind. The Vics eased the regulation as a temporary measure during World War Two but publicans forgot to sack them when the boys got back. Thank God.

Everyone has heard of the Eureka Stockade but in 1918 beer restrictions led to the most serious and prolonged civil disobedience campaign ever witnessed in Australia.

The Federal Government ran Darwin's hotels after World War One and imposed laws which restricted people taking beer away from pubs and then raised the price by threepence.

A boycott was declared and in December 1918, 1000 men stormed the administrator's office demanding the man be sent away on the first steamer. The administrator was manhandled, his assistant lost his trousers and an effigy was burnt. That administrator left town, as did another six months later, along with his secretary and the judge of the Supreme Court.

This was a serious issue and eventually the drinkers prevailed.

The answers to life's problems aren't at the bottom of a beer bottle, they're on TV.

Homer Simpson

BOB HAWKE'S RECORD

Politicians are remembered in history for all sorts of contributions: wars, corruption, sex scandals, economic mismanagement, taxes, total bastardry, ignorance, sloth, greed ... but one got his name in the textbooks for the right reason — beer drinking.

Our own Rhodes Scholar in Canberra, the right honourable former prime minister Bob Hawke actually made history even before he took the top job.

As a young man at Oxford, the knockabout soon-to-be union leader was called out at the dining hall of his college for not wearing a gown. As part of the college rules he was obliged to down two and a half pints of British ale in less than twenty-five seconds. According to Bob's memoirs, failure to do so meant he would have to pay for the first drink and then another.

Bob was a politician even in those days and didn't think he should have to fork out his own hard-earned money for a beer, so he took on that ale like his life depended upon it. Terrified of reaching into his pocket, the young Aussie student knocked back the lot in eleven seconds. The effort was recorded for history in the Guinness Book of Records.

Bob's record stood for some time, but we have heard about a young fellow called Leo Williams from the University of Queensland who put our Hawkie to shame. Representing the law faculty, the young man took on the whole campus in a drinking competition.

Leo almost broke the laws of physics by downing 2.6 litres in an incredible 7.9 seconds.

Apparently, a guy called Harold Fulton managed to drink thirty pints of beer in Sydney in the 1960s during an eight-hour session. He only had one leg too!

BREAKFAST OF CHAMPIONS

At any given time the sun is over the yardarm in some part of the world, but for brewers it's never too early to have a drink. These hearty souls not only make the beloved liquid, some include it in their breakfast.

Here's a little recipe for a brewer's breakfast. It's not quite hair of the dog, more of a lining for the kennel.

THE BREWER'S BREAKFAST
one bowl of toasted muesli
one cup of hot wort straight from the mash (unhopped)
half a cup of fruit
one cup of yoghurt

Pour into schooner glass, hold nose and drink in one swill.

CRICKETERS

Remember the great days of the Australian male? Remember when real men wore moustaches without fear of any confusion in a public toilet? Remember the Aussie bloke and his beer-drinking exploits? Remember our cricket side when every single bloke was a fair-dinkum-knockabout-larrikin who was pretty good on the field but much better in the pub?

Not that long ago the Australian cricket team made most builders' labourers look like synchronised swimmers. Back then the great challenge for our first XI wasn't facing the fearsome Windies, or even deciding which open-necked paisley shirt went with which slacks; no, it was how much beer you could drink.

And if the Ashes were the ultimate in cricketing tradition, then the Australia–England jet-plane beer-drinking record ran a close second.

For many years it was held by the laidback Doug Walters, a man who could knock up a ton, drop a bit of money at the races, and smoke half a pack of fags between lunch and tea.

It's alleged Doug once stunned the whole side by announcing he was going to 'warm up'. Nobody hated practice more than this naturally talented New South Welshman. Having made the statement, Doug arose, threw two darts at a dartboard, and sat down.

Warmed up.

In 1977 Doug Walters sat down for forty-four cans of beer on a flight between Sydney and London, a mark most considered unbeatable. Asked about this by *Inside Edge* magazine, Dougie told them a little about the flight.

'Rod and I used to sit together and have a drink on the plane. Now we got some good service in those days and we set some records that I don't think will be broken for a long while — you can't get that sort of service on a plane these days.'

Doug reckons it took a concentrated effort to establish the record and he didn't dare sleep.

'No way, mate. You can't sleep and drink at the same time.'

Then Rod Marsh, the West Australian wicket-keeper who looked like the progeny of a wrestler and a walrus, decided that he was going to set his own record. At five foot eight and a half inches, Marsh was heavy-set and had classic beer-drinker's legs: each one looked like it could — and on some occasions did — hold a keg of beer.

Rod always claimed that he had matched Doug beer for beer on the recordbreaking 1977 flight where he had acted as pace-maker, but nobody believed him. His chance to prove himself came in 1983 when the team was due to fly to London for the World Series in England.

Rod's best mate Dennis Lillee knew that the wicket-keeper was keen to have a crack, but secretly believed it wasn't a good idea. Now the fast bowler is no wowser himself, but he figured that it would be better to have somebody behind the stumps who hadn't died of alcoholic poisoning before landing in the Land of the Pom.

So, Dennis decided to get his mate well tanked before take-off. They drank on the red eye special all the way from Western Australia, kept going at an official cocktail party in Melbourne and then really hit their straps when they landed in Sydney the night before their departure for England.

The plan worked a treat and everybody was crook as a dog the next morning, but just to make sure, the fast bowler lured Rod in for a couple of dog hairs before the flight. Three to be exact — and they weren't to be counted as part of the trip.

To make an attempt on any record takes a lot of preparation and planning and this record was no exception. The flight took twenty-four hours in three legs: Sydney to Singapore, Singapore to Bahrain, and Bahrain to London. That's fifteen cans a leg and two cans an hour if you're going to beat the record.

Despite his mate's best attempts at sabotage, Rod pressed the hostie button the moment the wheels left the ground in Sydney. The hostess was informed of the plans and said that she would help in any way possible.

Apparently he was drinking Fosters, and although it sounded like he was speaking English as a second language, he was right on target when the plane touched down in Singapore. Graeme Wood was keeping score and had the little fella down for fifteen cans.

It was illegal to drink during refuelling — something to do with volatile fumes mixing with the avgas — and the moment they touched down Rod passed out.

Lillee relaxed; his plan had worked and his mate couldn't keep up the pace.

But he had underestimated the guy, who was one of the greatest keepers of all time, for the moment the plane was in the air again Rod was alert and drinking and put away fifteen more on the next leg.

In his book *Over and Out*, Lillee claims that he fell asleep on this leg and was horrified to wake in Bahrain and see that his mate had put away thirty cans. Admittedly Marshy was now talking in an obscure Arabian dialect, but like a good keeper, he hadn't missed a chance and was well on the way to the record.

When the plane touched down the little fella went quiet, apparently having passed out.

Of course, the moment that old plane took off Rod was back at it again and by this time the whole economy section was following the mammoth innings taking place high in the skies above the northern hemisphere. This was Bradmanesque — not that the teetotalling Don would have approved.

Even the captain joined in and made an announcement about the record attempt to those who hadn't already caught on. In those days responsible service of alcohol meant you could serve anybody who could remember their name or knew somebody who once remembered their name. Back then the only time you were too drunk to drive was when you couldn't find your car; and our man had no intention of driving anywhere, so they just kept those beers coming.

Anyway, the tally kept rising and Lillee swears that as the plane tilted for its descent towards Heathrow, beer started to spill over his mate's bottom teeth.

As they approached the airport, can forty-four arrived and was eventually forced down before tragedy struck. The record-breaking forty-fifth can came down the aisle and somehow Marsh indicated that he couldn't do it. The runway was approaching almost as fast as the ignominious failure.

Back in those days a mate was a real mate and the rest of the team held his mouth open and somehow poured the beer down his throat. Although, if the truth be known it probably came to rest about a centimetre below his tonsils.

Rod Marsh had done it and there were delirious celebrations from everybody except the wicket-keeper, who was by now catatonic.

Woods and Lillee had to change him out of his drinking clothes and into the official ACB gear before hitting customs. They propped him between themselves and made for the gates, only to be caught by the lizards of the English press who had the temerity to suggest in the next day's paper that Lillee had been in on the game too.

If they only knew what a wowser he really was.

But there you have it — Rod Marsh, beer-drinking champion of the Australian cricket team with an unbeaten forty-five-can London–Heathrow record.

Many claim David Boon later matched or beat this, but Boon denies it and we can find no reason to doubt him. Cricketers don't lie. Do they?

Merv Hughes says that Boonie knocked off fifty-six cans on a flight to London. Walters argues that Boon is not in the running for the record because he counted the ones he drank in the terminal.

Boonie spoke about the record recently and said that it was 'a fairytale'. When asked how many he really had he said, 'Oh mate, you can make whatever mark you want. When you're having a beer, who counts?'

Why don't Channel Nine do a commemorative print of the lads' famous feats? There'd be plenty who'd be proud to hang that on the wall of the home bar. I can hear Tony Greig's sales pitch now: 'This wonderful commemorative print captures the moment the ...' Oh well, maybe not.

AUSTRALIA TO LONDON UNOFFICIAL BEER-DRINKING RECORDS

Year	Name	Cans
1977	Doug Walters	44 cans
1983	Rodney Marsh	45 cans
1993	David Boon	56 cans (unconfirmed)

DEAD DRUNK

There's a story doing the rounds about a thirty-three-year-old Australian who won some sort of drinking contest, but at enormous cost.

This bloke, who worked in the computing industry but didn't have quite as many megabytes of hard drive as you'd expect, keeled over after drinking thirty-four glasses of beer, four bourbons and sixteen tequilas in one hour and forty minutes. His blood alcohol was apparently .353. That's more than seven times over the limit and way past a man's ability to keep alive, let alone drive.

Our computer geek was partaking in a drinking competition which gave contestants 100 minutes in which to consume as much alcohol as possible. Under the rules of the competition, you were awarded one point for a beer, three for a wine and eight for a spirit. Our man scored 202 — the equivalent of 202 beers in 100 minutes — and won the competition by 44 points.

Unfortunately, he died before he could collect the prize and the barman was fined $20,000 for his part in the stupidity.

The difference between a drunk and an alcoholic is that a drunk doesn't have to attend all those meetings.

Arthur Lewis

FISHY STORY

Believe it or not, anthropologists believe the human race has survived until now because it drank beer.

Back in the time when water was a carrier of the Black Plague and all sorts of disease, even the churches recommended that people drink ale (the only known beer in the early days). Apart from the fact that the church owned the breweries, they also knew that the water in it was boiled and sterilised.

Anthropologists reckon that people in the West developed a capacity for grog during these times, while the gene pools of Asia were saved by a taste for tea, which is apparently also made from boiled water.

The earliest recorded mentions of beer date back to 6000BC. There's even some thought that civilisation began when the old-timers began to harvest the first crops — in order to make bread and beer. The words have the same origin and beer was once made after the grains were baked into a bread-like form which was then able to be soaked in liquid.

While it would have been pretty rough to drink and people probably used straws to filter the crap out, at least it kept you alive and happy. Some time later people realised that bread filled in a few gaps as well.

These days the water's clean, except that fish fornicate in it, and now it appears that there could even be fish and pig gut in beer. Animal liberationists, People for the Ethical Treatment of Animals, recently launched a campaign warning that some beers contain pepsin, a protein from pigs' stomachs that makes beer frothy.

There is also a concern that brewers are using fish bladders to clean the impurities. And they're right; there's a product called Isinglass, made from fish bladders, which is used to remove the yeast from beer.

Now you know!

MEATY DROP

A lot of good beers and breweries have come and gone since white man first built a pub on these shores. Then again, a lot of forgettable crap has gone the same way.

One brewer wrote to the *Australian Beer Journal* in March 1895 with details of his remarkable new recipe for an ale which he claimed 'will be a valuable medium for supplying nourishment to persons who are in ill health and unable to take food in its solid form'.

Yeah, right.

The brewer's recipe involved adding fifteen pounds of calves' heads or feet, ten pounds of bullocks' heads and shins of beef, two bushels of malt, twelve pounds of hops and five grains of quinine to every brew.

One can only imagine that a vegetarian plot undermined this ingenious recipe and stopped it becoming as Australian for beer as, well, you know.

Beer is proof that God loves us and wants us to be happy.

Benjamin Franklin

PUB WITH NO BEER

Everybody has heard the song, but did you know it is based on a real-life tragedy?

There have been some dark days in Australian history, but none so bleak as that terrible time that Ingham boy Dan Sheahan arrived at the Day Dawn Hotel after a hard day's work only to be greeted with the news that the pub had no beer as American servicemen had drunk it dry.

The Yanks' troop convoys had passed through town and shown scant regard for the quota system which was in place at the time because of the war. And they were supposed to be on our side!

With a tear in his eye, Dan accepted a glass of wine and retired forlornly to the parlour and began to write a poem.

The late Gordon Parsons, singer-songwriter and timber worker from the Kempsey area, changed the lyrics a little and set them to the tune of an 1862 American folk song by Stephen Collins Foster called 'Beautiful Dreamer'.

Slim Dusty recorded the song 'The Pub With No Beer' and the rest is history ... well, almost.

You can find The Pub With No Beer at Taylor's Arms, near Kempsey, New South Wales, but Queenslanders reckon that Ingham's Lee Hotel, which is on the site of the old Day Dawn Hotel, is the real McCoy.

RUSSIA AILED BY BEER

You've got to love those Russians; they just seem to have a thirst for the hard stuff that leaves most of us looking like bloody great nancies.

In January 2001 the Russian Health Ministry launched a campaign for beer to be recognised as an alcoholic drink. For some strange reason the Russkis never considered the amber stuff to be alcoholic and so even children could buy and drink it.

The idea was that if it was readily available people would drink less vodka, but it seems the locals just drank vodka and beer.

The mayor of Moscow even authorised the building of a large brewery outside the city saying that beer was the perfect cure for recovering alcoholics.

Sounds like the sort of politician we need.

WAR STORIES

A BELLYFUL
Butch Brown

During my first tour of duty in Vietnam (1967–68) we were under the old rule of one beer per man per day. In an effort to 'savour' the event, we would drink them a little faster than normal and then lie down on the sandbag bunkers and let the sun warm up the belly.

After a few minutes you would stand up very fast. The reaction was like that of smoking your first cigarette and getting very dizzy. Short-lived, but something to look forward to the next day!

A CASE OF VD
Brian Wallace

A navy ship had been in an exotic port for a couple of weeks when the captain ordered all the crew together.

'Gentlemen, I am disturbed to have to say that we have discovered quite a few cases of VD on board the ship,' he said.

'That's good,' said one of the sailors.

'What could be good about that?' asked the captain.

'Well,' said the sailor, 'it's got to be better than the local beer.'

A FOSTERS OR AN ABBOTTS
Neil Gillies

I was serving with 6th Battery, 2/3rd Field Regiment and at our first position in Greece we were issued with two bottles of beer. The signals sergeant did the issuing but had some bottles left over as they couldn't be sent to observation posts etc.

When we were forced to withdraw, some infantry men stopped and gave covering fire while our guns were timbered up, then hopped onto our trucks. A couple got into a signals van. One of them said, 'How'd a beer go now?' and nearly fell out of the van when a sig produced two bottles and said, 'Which one do you want, a Fosters or an Abbotts?'

BEER PYRAMID
Fred Fortescue

I was in the RAAF in Vietnam (Caribou Transport Flight at Vung Tau) in the very early days of our involvement in the war (June 1965). Our access to any beer other than the local 333 was nil.

As secretary of our little 'club' at the villa I had heard that in Saigon the Americans had a warehouse full of beer (used to supply their Special Forces camps).

So, armed with a fistful of US dollars and a helper, and with the cooperation of the pilot of one of our Caribous, it was arranged that we (and the beer — about sixty cartons) would be picked up at the Ton-Son-Aut (Saigon airport) at about 4 p.m. one afternoon.

Everything went very well and we were in position on the tarmac at 2 p.m. with the beer.

We couldn't leave our prize, but to fill in the time my helper suggested we build a sort of pyramid out of all the cartons. It looked great.

At 3.30 p.m. a tropical rain storm hit us and dumped approx one and a half feet of water on us and the pyramid of cartons. There was hardly a carton which was not soaked. Our Caribou arrived on time and we loaded the beer a can at a time, as each carton fell apart as soon as you touched it.

The unloading at Vung Tau was the same — one can at a time out of the plane and one at a time into a truck and again a can at a time at the villa.

The beer by now was hot and undrinkable due to the way it had been thrown about. After we'd chilled the beer (for twenty-four hours) everyone enjoyed a better-quality brew.

I did the same trip to the Saigon warehouse every two weeks for the next six months, except I had a very heavy large tarpaulin and a helper who was content to sit on a square block of cartons for however long it took.

KOREAN HOPSICLES
Dudley C Pye

During the Christmas of 1953 I was a young soldier/cook serving in Korea. The practice of the government was to issue soldiers with a beer ration on days such as Christmas Day, ANZAC Day etc.

Two bottles of Abbotts lager were issued per soldier for Christmas Day; they were to be consumed with lunch in an effort to improve morale.

The intense cold (minus fifteen degrees centigrade) caused the beer to become somewhat frozen and great difficulty was experienced in attempting to consume the much anticipated brew.

As it was so cold, many soldiers were gathered around my field stove and some bottles were placed on top of the range where the bottoms became heated a little. Soon the heat began to force the beer up through the neck of the bottles like a candle-shaped periscope.

The diggers then proceeded to chew lumps from the beer candles as they rose from the bottle like some kind of hopsicle. As the beer warmed too much, the bottle was placed in the snow to refreeze and the process was repeated.

What a Christmas! And those memories are recalled each ANZAC Day as the tastiest Christmas candles ever invented.

This now old cook still likes a cold drop on a hot day.

Always do sober what you said you'd do drunk. That will teach you to keep your mouth shut.

Ernest Hemingway

UNOPENED BEER AND DUNNY DOORS
Andrew McCarthy

Back in the early 1970s when I was serving on HMAS *Melbourne*, our mess had a soft drink fridge. Cartons of soft drink were purchased ashore and the fridge was kept full of various types. Payment for each drink was via an honesty box and any profits went towards a mess party at some overseas port.

Before leaving Sydney for exercises off Hawaii I was elected to be drinks purchaser and I duly purchased large quantities of Tarax Black Label drinks (now there's a blast from the past).

At Pearl Harbor I went off to the local PX to restock our supplies and was confronted by a number of brand names that I hadn't heard of. I purchased cartons at random, later carrying them as bold as brass with a few of the blokes up the gangway and down into the mess.

At sea a couple of days later, we discovered that the lemonade in the flashy blue cartons was in fact PABST beer. Needless to say it was secreted away — smuggling booze on board was a big no no — to be enjoyed on the last night before hitting Sydney.

And what a night it was.

When at sea on *Melbourne*, each man was entitled to one 26oz (750ml) can a day, provided there was no night flying that night.

We were in a petty officers mess (senior sailors) and as such a couple of mess members would collect a can for every member. Any non-drinker's can would be stored away for the last night party before getting home.

The powers that be were aware of these lurks and when they were collected the cans were 'cracked' (back in the days of the ring pull). This was always done for junior sailors, but it was overlooked for senior sailors as a sort of unofficial privilege of rank.

This practice came to the attention of a very strict and straight 'Master at Arms' (the ship's head policeman) nicknamed The Hat (sailors from the 1970s will know who he was). The Hat ordered that senior sailors' cans were to be 'cracked' before issue. This almost caused a mutiny amongst us and there was much bitching and moaning.

I can remember one old salt saying that the only privilege senior sailors had on this ship was 'unopened cans of beer and longer shithouse doors!' (junior sailors had half length doors, senior sailors three-quarter length and officers full length).

The next morning some wag got hold of a texta and drew dotted lines on the doors of the senior sailors' toilets (heads) near our mess, with the words 'cut here'.

HOME-BREWERS

A BEERY CONFESSION
Anonymous

In the late 1970s I worked for a large company in Sydney. During our lunch breaks a lot of the men got together in the canteen (or sometimes down the local). The conversation varied from sport to eating and drinking.

At the time home-brewing was big in the suburbs, particularly among the married men. Being single, I had better things to do with my time and money.

Naturally each person reckoned his brew was the best and tasted like the real thing. They often brought samples for me to try. Not wishing to offend, I told them it was hard to tell the difference; home-brew is home-brew — and nothing has changed if you ask me.

Anyway, the boys decided they would have a home-brew barbecue at Browny's place. Everyone had to bring six 750ml bottles of their finest for judging by the experts.

Not wanting to be left out, I put down a brew from one of the many recipes given to me. I'll be honest: it was nearly undrinkable.

On the day of the big event, I bought three large bottles of KB and three bottles of Tooheys Flag Ale, removed the labels and replaced the tops with my plain crown seals.

For a start my two beers caught everyone's eye because there was no sediment; the old-style home-brews were loaded with it.

Then the taste really got to them.

I was going to own up at the end of the day but I got in so deep with all my secrecy and fibs that I had to go on with it.

For months after the event my brews were discussed reverently and my mates tried to make me give up my secrets, but to no avail.

I no longer have contact with those guys so you can let 'Feet's' secret out of the bag if you want — sorry Browny and the Eveready Gang.

I hope you will forgive me.

BAD OLD DAYS
Kevin J Crouch

Mine is a vintage tale dating back to the late 1940s, not long after World War Two, when beer was scarce indeed. These were the heady days of the 'six o'clock swill', when if you didn't tip the barmaid threepence a drink at the rare hours when the beer was 'on', you became invisible and didn't get another drink.

Bottled beer was a ration of two bottles per week, but only if you were a regular and qualified for a voucher.

My friend Bob and I decided to brew our own to save all the running around from pub to pub, only to find when you got there that the keg had just run out and there was no more. We were single young blokes and Bob's parents lived at the time in a short street that backed on to the Royal Manly Golf Course.

Bob and I resided in the garage at the back of Bob's parents' house, where we set up our own 'brewery': two four-gallon kerosene tins with the tops cut out held our special brew. On waking each morning, our first job was to inspect the magic potion and scoop off any mosquito wrigglers that had made their appearance overnight. When we considered it ready to bottle, we did so with the recommended amount of sugar and stored it in the cool under the main house for a couple of weeks.

Approaching the first bottle with some trepidation, we found it was drinkable, which was about the best that could be said of it.

Some well-meaning soul told us to double the sugar in the next batch, because this would give it 'a bit of a kick' and make it taste better. So we did just that.

We stored it under the house in the usual manner. However, one night Bob's mum came down to the garage, woke us and said, 'Whatever's going on with your beer I don't know, but there is a lot of noise. It woke me up. Please go and have a look.'

Sadly, most of our bottles had self-destructed and the area was an unholy mess. That was our last attempt at home-brewing.

Good old days, my eye! Now we can sample wonderful beers from all over the country, all over the world for that matter. I have been fortunate enough to have been able to sample many beers from many countries, without ever having left Sydney and its environs. In my opinion, some of our own beers must rate with the world's best: Squires, Dogbolter, Moonshine (Victorian) and Balmain Bock (which I hear is no longer brewed), to name only a few which come to mind. Our wonderful brewers in this country have produced lots more which I anticipate tasting before I fall off the perch.

CAT-A-TONIC
Ken Evans

I've seen beer do strange things to men and women, but nothing like what it did to our family cats.

Patch and Ribs (mother and son) were feline residents and part of our family, commanding full attention as to food requirements and hours of leisure. In fact, leading a perfect cat's life.

I was in my learning mode for home-brewing a few years back and had obtained all the ingredients separately, mixing up a concoction from a recipe given to me by someone who knew someone who knew something about home-brewing. Or at least that was the story. This was in the days before home-brew shops and kits.

For this particular brew I decided to put half in 750ml bottles and half in 375ml stubbies. For some bizarre reason (I wonder if it had anything to do with beer) my teenage son begged to help me and after I recovered from the shock I put him in charge of adding the sugar prior to bottling and gave him precise instructions on how to do it.

Task completed, we put the bottles onto shelves in the external laundry for the secondary fermentation. Coincidentally, this was Patch and Ribs' boudoir.

Two weeks after bottling the brew I went into the laundry to let the cats out for the day. An unusual sight confronted me. Two cats, oblivious to their surroundings, were walking at virtually half their normal height, scraping the ground, their eyes glazed, racing in forward motion with only their toes moving (the same as cartoon cats on the TV), desperate to escape as quickly as possible from their house of horrors.

Evidently through the night the 375ml stubbies, due to their thin glass walls, had been unable to hold the inner pressure and had exploded, causing a chain reaction, smashing about six bottles. Glass shards and beer was everywhere.

Imagine what it had been like for Patch and Ribs, settled in for the night when all of a sudden all hell breaks loose. It was Pearl Harbor in the laundry and they had no way of escaping and no idea about what was happening.

They were in shock — literally out of their minds with fear.

What caused the bottles to erupt?

My son had done what he thought was right and put the same amount of sugar into each bottle, causing a vigorous secondary fermentation in the smaller bottles. Who said teenagers don't listen?

The poor cats were not keen to sleep in the laundry that night; in fact, they even discovered a hitherto unknown ability to run backwards in order to escape.

Soon after, Patch died after being run over by the family car, although it was thought this might have been suicide. Ribs died of kidney failure.

It seemed neither had the will to go on. Talk about having the horrors!

EXPLODING BEER BOTTLES
Elaine Johnston

Everybody has heard about the Japanese attacks on Darwin and the invasion of Sydney Harbour during World War Two by mini submarine, but a few of us were involved in a little-known battle in our suburban street.

During World War Two, our next-door neighbour made quantities of home-brew which he stored under the house. Late one night, loud explosions rocked the street. Our family and many neighbours raced into our backyard and down into our large air-raid shelter.

We huddled in the dark, fearing the 'invasion' had begun. During a long silence, some of the men ventured out and discovered smashed bottles and tops — the 'bombs' were cases of home-brew exploding amongst the foundations and against the floorboards.

Talk of 'having a beer' was greeted by sheepish grins and laughter for some time afterwards. (But, of course, a lot of beer had to be 'disposed of' — read that as 'consumed' — in a hurry 'in case it goes off again, mate!')

HARD TO SWALLOW
Brian Noyes

I was having a drink with this home-brewer at the local pub when the publican called last drinks.

We'd put a few away but needed a roadie to clear the head. This was in the bad old days when bottle shops closed earlier than banks and it was looking pretty bleak.

Jim — well, that's what I'll call him in an attempt to keep his guilt anonymous — suggested I go back home and try one of his home-brews.

Now, other blokes had done this in the past and those that had survived the experience described a drink that while alcoholic was so bad not even the most hardened alcoholic could come near more than one. It had the odour of month-old witches' knickers and a flavour not unlike the slops that you find at the bottom of an abattoir's wheelie bin after a hot day.

I must've been a bit more pithed than I thought because somehow I found myself on the way back to Jim's house.

His horrible old wife greeted us at the door with a face that would scare Mike Tyson and an order that we take ourselves out to the back shed and not bother her or her equally ugly sister. Fat chance of that.

Anyway, Jim was also pleased to be banished to the shed and so we slunk through the house and made for the backyard.

Out in the shed he opened the fridge like a man opening a treasure chest. I swear the bottles were squirming and seething on the shelves and there appeared to be a foul green gas rising through the corroding tops.

Jim grabbed a bottle and then reached in the drawer for a bottle opener and a gun.

Yes, a gun.

Shit, I thought, he's gonna kill me.

'Don't be frightened,' said Jim. 'This is just to make sure we both have a nice drink.'

I was absolutely petrified as I didn't really

know him that well and I was even more scared when he poured out a huge glass of this bubbling, burping, stenching, farting liquid and told me it was all mine.

'I, I, I, I might have lost me thirst, mate,' I said. 'I think I might've copped a poison pizza back at the pub.'

Jim went all strange and quiet. He looked at me, pulled the hammer back on the gun and pointed it at my temple.

'Drink the beer,' he said.

Trembling and gagging I raised the glass to my lips and apologised to God for being such a useless specimen, adding that I would never again get drunk, ignore the wife or ogle women if He let me out of this spot.

God is a bastard and I was forced to knock back the home-brew. Knowing not to sip, I threw it all down in one gulp.

I started to shake and sweat and everything spun for a while, but somehow I stayed on my feet and, despite feeling like a rat was decomposing in my stomach, I realised I was going to live.

Jim looked quite pleased about this and seemed to relax.

'Okay,' he said. 'Now it's your turn to hold the gun while I have a glass.'

HOMIES
Peter Lalor

Hidden in sheds and cellars around this beer-loving country is a strange breed of man, and the odd woman. Like mad scientists they hover over steaming vats, mix strange-smelling exotic potions, and pace the boards anxiously waiting for their creations to take life.

They are home-brewers and they are not like other people. They're obsessive, devoted, generally bloated and usually pretty bloody good people.

Up Bathurst way there is a thriving gang of homies who are so dedicated to beer that you'd think they had discovered a new religion. Come to think of it, the Church of Beer would have some appeal!

The treasurer of the Bathurst club, Big John, is a man who knows that a good brewer needs to be able to control his fermentation and lagering temperatures. In Bathurst the mercury is up and down more often than a unisex toilet seat and so something had to be done to keep Big John's brews in good shape.

Sparing no expense, he went out and bought a top of the range air conditioner and had it fitted to the small shed by the carport.

The only problem was, Big John's long-suffering missus had sweltered through the last thirty years in the house with only an electric fan for her comfort! Anyway, she soon got over it and was even allowed to go out and sit with the beer when the heat became too unbearable.

John, like the others, has converted a fridge into a mini pub. The boys just drill two holes in the door, fit taps and load the kegs inside. It's the perfect way to serve beer as you don't even have to open the fridge to get another coldie.

Another one of the homies, G, who hangs out with the Bathurst crew, bears the scars of his love for homemade beer. One night G was carrying a glass carboy filled with the precious fluid when it overbalanced and began to fall from his arms.

Now, a true disaster was on the cards.

No, G wasn't concerned about getting out of the way of the soon to be shattered glass that would surely explode like a bomb because of the gas inside; he was just keen to save what was apparently a top little ale and so he made a desperate lunge to save the batch.

Unfortunately, he failed and the breaking glass slashed his wrists and throat and he almost bled to death. Still, greater love hath no man …

You can imagine what sort of fishing trips the boys from the Bathurst home-brew club take. There's an absolute s——load of rods, reels, camping gear, food — and then there's the beer.

These blokes take two industrial-size freezers, a generator and on average about two kegs per man. Two blokes are on full-time bar duties roster and are expected to keep the beer in tip-top shape and make sure the lines and glasses are clean.

One of these years the boys reckon they might even catch a fish.

LOLLYWATER
Ray Hardes

A friend of mine, we'll call him B2 to protect his identity, recently went on holidays and left the keys to his shed with a good friend. We borrowed a bottle of B2's home-brew, drank the beer and replaced the beer with cold tea and put the bottle back in his shed fridge.

After B2 had returned from holidays he was telling me that he had taken a few home-brews around to a friend's place at the weekend.

He said his friend keeps his beer glasses in the freezer and when he poured the beer it partly froze and tasted like lollywater.

'I don't know what went wrong, but I could not drink it,' said B2.

I managed to keep a straight face during all this and B2 did not suspect any foul play.

A week later, a group of us were playing cards and I took out a bottle of cold tea from the fridge.

When I poured it into B2's glass, he tasted it and said, 'Hey, the same thing must have happened to your beer.'

The problem with the world is that everyone is a few drinks behind.

Humphrey Bogart

MOTHBALLS
Paulene Lowe

Times were pretty tough during the war years for most families and ours was no exception, what with Mum, Dad and five kids to feed.

My dad always loved his beer, so he took to making his first home-brew. I believe it was a potent brew and we were forbidden to go into the back shed, as Dad would bravely enter each day to check how many bottles had exploded.

Six to eight weeks later the big tasting took place. Friends were invited in true Aussie tradition — everything was shared in those days.

There was great excitement as Dad poured everyone a drink and one for himself and Mum. As everybody took a sip a deathly silence descended and then someone mentioned mothballs, then another, then another.

Apparently in those days, at some stage you had to strain the brew. Mum had got out one of the clean blankets for the process, forgetting that she had stored the blankets in mothballs.

No one seemed to mind the mothballs taste as every last bottle was opened and drunk. I remember there were some massive headaches, but everyone lived to a ripe old age and kept coming to visit our home.

Forget the dot coms, the Internet, rockets to the moon. Remember good old Aussie tradition — a good beer, a barbecue and great friends. Our son is carrying on the tradition: he makes his own home-brew.

A great drop — without the mothballs.

NIGHTCAP
Jim Ratcliffe

We own the Home-Brew Shop (and barbers) at Kincumber on the Central Coast and naturally get some funny tales from our customers.

Bill, one of our customers, had just started to make home-brew, but he found his first brew was too bitter, so instead of adding one kilogram of sugar he used two. This would achieve nothing, as the sugar converts to alcohol; he should have lowered the amount of hops. So the brew got stronger but not sweeter.

The beer was still too bitter for Bill so he added three kilos of sugar to his next brew, making it three times stronger.

When I asked Bill if the beer was any good he replied, 'Very good, only my wife insists that I put on my pyjamas and sit on the bed before I can have a schooner so she can just roll me over and cover me when I have finished my beer.'

When I read
about the evils of
drinking, I gave up
reading.

Henny Youngman

OH DEAR, NO BEER
Hayden MacKellar

What a horrible feeling to be left without beer after a lousy day and, worse yet, being unable to buy any to rectify the situation.

Recently I had the pleasure of moving house and all our worldly possessions to a new suburb that we did not know very well. The weekend, which happened to be the Easter long weekend, had proved to be ideal.

I had enlisted two willing friends to help with the worst of the load with a reward of cold beer and a seafood lunch. After several round trips and plenty of effort, we had managed to get the job done without too much drama and all in time for the lunch I had promised.

All the seafood was ready, as were the appetites, but when I looked in the Esky for some beer to offer my friends I remembered that during all the packing up I had given away the remainder of my beer supply, thinking I would resupply rather than heave it during the move.

I was stunned and also embarrassed that I suddenly had nothing to offer my hired help. As it was Good Friday afternoon, I also realised I had absolutely no chance of buying any, no matter how desperate we were or how far I drove.

Enter the new next-door neighbour, who came by to introduce herself and had in her hand a plastic bag holding four longnecks of her husband's home-brew. It had high alcohol, a moderate head and was nice and cold.

I couldn't believe our luck. It was a just reward for the work we had done.

I have since replaced the beer to our generous neighbours and I have taken measures so I am never in that situation again, and I am always looking to extend my collection.

THE POSTIE
John Gibbins

Home-brewing was popular in Sydney in the early 1950s. This was necessary to cope with the yearly Christmas beer shortages due to strike action by the unions seeking pay increases.

My father was reasonably good at the art, having been supplied with the proper ingredients, recipes and working instructions by a friend who happened to be one of the striking workers from Reschs brewery. Dad was popular with the neighbours, as he became the source of the only amber fluid to be had locally.

However, his fame was short-lived with the local postman, who said he would have 'contemplated murder' if he could have escaped uncaught.

Let me continue ...

Postmen in those days did not zoom around on little Hondas; they had to make two mail deliveries daily on a push bike with a large leather mailbag over the front handle bars. It was customary for residents to give small Christmas gifts to the likes of the postman and garbage collectors for their diligent service throughout the year.

You guessed it — my father gave the postman two of his best brews. According to the postman's report the following day, both bottles exploded in his large leather mailbag after he had travelled less than 200 yards from our front gate. Ballpoint pens did not exist then and the ink-written addresses on the Christmas card envelopes had run.

The postman said he spent the rest of the day trying to dry out the envelopes and decipher the blurred addresses and NO he did not want the beer replaced. My dad never fails to recollect the story — 'Do you remember the postman blah, blah, blah' — as he samples my latest home-brewing effort.

AUSSIES ABROAD

A BLESSED LIFE
Greg Rieper

I was on my first overseas flight, sitting in economy (a row of three seats). I was in the window seat, next to me was a Catholic priest and next to him was a Pakistani, who was a Muslim. We'd had several conversations when the subject of alcohol was raised and, most importantly, beer and religion.

The Pakistani asked the priest if he was permitted to drink beer.

The priest replied, 'It would be a bloody dull life if we didn't.'

BLIND DRUNK
Mark Dennis

On a trip to Europe back in 1983 we were staying in a caravan park near Hamburg. After getting settled we went to visit the nearby bottle shop and after much deliberation we decided to buy two cartons of 500ml stubbies of beer.

There were four of us and we were attracted by the novelty value of a half-litre stubby and the fact that it was the cheapest beer in the shop.

A party awaited!

We got back to the caravan park later that afternoon and started drinking and did not stop until the wee hours of the morning when almost all the beer was gone. The beer had contributed to a good night and we all slept like logs.

On waking the next day, all feeling a little seedy and sheepish, we'd started to clean up the empty bottles when the caretaker approached. We thought we might be in trouble for drinking all night, but the bloke just cleared his throat and said in broken English, 'Well done, you've probably just broken some sort of beer-drinking record. I've never seen anybody drink so much non-alcoholic beer.'

To say there were four red-faced travellers was an understatement.

COLLECTING GLASSES
Kevin Bradley

My favourite beer yarn happened while my wife and I were touring Europe. We'd been travelling all over the continent enjoying foreign beers and, of course, collecting the usually quite decorative glass (as you do).

Whilst in Rome we went to a quaint little cafe and bar to enjoy a Peroni Nastro Azzurro or three. The glass looked quite collectable and it had my name written all over it. So I told my wife to whack this glass into her handbag, then we quickly left. Quite quickly, I might add.

Anyway, we'd gone about fifty metres down the road when the waiter came running after us, shouting something in Italian.

We looked at each other and thought, 'Should we run or face the consequences? I mean, what could they do? It's only a glass and we're dumb tourists who don't understand.' So we stood our ground.

The waiter came scurrying towards us talking very quickly in Italian. We were very worried.

Then from behind his back he pulled out our camera which we'd left behind in the rush.

We thanked him in the only Italian we knew — a tip.

We both heaved a big sigh of relief — but my wife gave me a serve over leaving the $400 camera for a $2 glass.

Work is the curse of the drinking classes.

Oscar Wilde

COLOUR BLIND
Gerard Meares

Being fortunate enough to be twenty years old and travelling Europe, we decided we should not neglect our education. In no time at all we had become experts in all things beer: Czech beer, German beer, Belgian beer, Irish beer. We saw every day as a chance to learn and try something new.

So there we were in Paris, half a dozen Aussies, well behaved, some may have even described us as pleasant company. Well, someone thought so, as we found ourselves invited to — of all things — a wine tasting.

We went. We tasted some wines and generally tried to fit in; that is, until Rob decided to ask a question.

No harm in that, but when he wanted to say 'Is this a dry or a sweet wine?' Rob came out with 'Is this a red or a white wine?'

We left not long after that, found a pub we hadn't been thrown out of and enjoyed yet another wonderful evening helped along by good beer and great friends.

To this day none of us drink wine!

FOR GOD'S SAKE
Jaak Jarv

Back in the middle of the 1970s I was in Belgium starting a new office for the company. Apart from Australia we also had offices in Houston, Texas and Tokyo, Japan at that stage.

One of the 'Good Old Boys' from the Houston office had cause to come over to Brussels for a period and one day we drove to Amsterdam to see a potential customer. We did whatever business we had to do and drove back to Brussels.

A kilometre or three from where we were living was a typical Belgian pub and we stopped there on the way home for a beer for the two of us.

The 'Good Old Boy' insisted on ordering, which he did in a loud voice: 'Dieu bieres s'il vous plait.'

To which the barman replied in excellent English, 'You have just ordered God's beer.'

Quick as a flash the 'GOB' was back with, 'I know — for God's sake give us a beer.'

GUINNESS FOR MOTHERS
Max van den Berg

The year 1982 was a very exciting time for my wife and me as it represented for us a series of firsts. Our first big holidays since we were married, the first time meeting our cousins and relatives, and the first time we had ever flown in an aeroplane. As one can imagine, we were in a state of great excitement by the time we boarded the plane at Mascot and after some six stopovers and thirty hours in the air we arrived at our destination — Holland.

This holiday on the other side of the globe was filled with excitement and wonderment and, given the short length of our vacation, we endeavoured to make every post a winner.

Having come so far, one of the absolute musts was to take a journey to the place of my mother's people, that being Ireland. Just getting to the Emerald Isle produced more stories than one might imagine, but the one I wish to recount occurred in County Clare.

Having arrived in Ireland we caught a train to our initial destination, where we established our home base in Mrs B Feeney's Bed and Breakfast, County Limerick. Following a minimum rest period we set about planning the best way to approach this fabled County Clare, given the limited resources at our disposal — namely, an empty pot of gold.

After considering our options it was agreed that we would travel in the most economical (and Irish) way possible: on shanks's pony. So, with purposeful strides we set off to discover the neighbouring county. According to the locals it was going to be one of those beautiful Irish occasions when the sun was to shine for the entire day, so consequently we were able to travel with a minimum amount of baggage, or in my case, garbage, as my wife would say. We walked for what seemed an eternity and by early afternoon our thoughts were beginning to remind us of the amount of slogging that would be required to complete the return journey.

On winding our way back to our lodging we passed a rather quaint little inn set well back from the road that had taken our fancy when we had passed it earlier in the day. Since I was yet to experience the sensation of a true glass of Irish Guinness stout I put forward the idea that given the circumstances I might break the drought in the inviting arms of the little tavern.

'But Max, we still have so far to go. Can't it wait until we get back to town?'

To this day I'm not sure how, but my body language must have suggested the urgency of my plea for I found myself leading my wife through the wooden doors of the pub without further protest.

Upon entering the premises we found the interior had both warmth and charm, with its heavily timbered walls and ceilings adding a feeling of grandeur associated with days gone by. A fine collection of Irish males was gathered around the bar, neatly attired in Donegal tweed coats and hats, who, we imagined, were completely oblivious to our presence as they continued on unabated in their various discussions.

We must have appeared like a pair of novices for as I was seating my wife at one of the tables a voice from behind caught my attention and I turned around to be greeted by a jovial Irish gentleman holding two pints of Guinness in his hands.

'Pat McNally's the name and I saw how you were both visitors [we must have stood out like sore thumbs] and how your lovely wife here is expecting [indeed, she was about six months expecting] so I'd like to say "Welcome to Ireland" and I want you to have a drink on me, particularly as your wife is expecting, 'cause y'know Guinness is good for mothers in child.'

With that he promptly left the drinks on the table and returned to the bar.

This gracious gesture on the part of our new-found Irish friend caused considerable alarm for my wife as she would never partake of anything stronger than the occasional glass of dinner wine and as a matter of course had chosen not to drink any alcohol during her months of confinement.

'But, Yvonne,' I protested, 'Pat would be offended if you refused his gesture of kindness. Look, you're just going to have to make the effort.'

After much deliberation and staring at the container my wife raised the glass to her lips and took a sip. The expression that came over her face suggested to me that she might be about to give birth right then and there.

'My God,' she choked. 'I'll just die if I have to drink this stuff.'

That terminated any further discussion on the subject.

Conscious of the need to satisfy custom and keep my marriage on the rails I made the bold suggestion that I would quickly drink my glass of Guinness and while no one was watching attempt the old 'switch-a-roo' and exchange glasses with my wife, thereby satisfying all parties.

Unfortunately for me someone was watching, for the next thing I knew there stood good old Pat with two more pints of Ireland's best.

'Pat, you shouldn't,' I protested. 'Really, we are very grateful for your kindness but we can't keep taking advantage of your hospitality like this.'

Pat would have none of this and after placing the drinks in front of us returned to be enveloped in the smoke and din that was being played out at the other end of the bar.

The scenario of the black medicine being good for mother and child routine was to go around two more times before the old 'switch-a-roo' was replaced with feelings of 'straight-to-the-loo'. With the double-barrelled prospect of an all-in domestic coupled with acute kidney failure, a joint decision (she decided, I complied) was taken and come hell or high water my wife was leaving.

It was then that the term 'legless' demonstrated its true meaning, for unlike my sober wife, whose path didn't deviate one step as she approached the door, my attempt at navigation resulted in my careering into every conceivable obstruction (including a now barking dog which had been sleeping under one of the tables).

Witnessing the untimely exit our friend Pat raced to the door to bid us farewell and, after the standard practice of exchanging information and addresses, took my hand and shook it vigorously and uttered these words that will live in my mind forever.

'Well, Max and Yvonne, it's been a pleasure to meet you and you never know, one day our paths may cross each other's again. But I've got to say one thing to you, Max, before you go — I don't know about you Australian men, but begorrah your women sure know how to hold their liquor!'

I am a drinker with writing problems.

Brendan Behan

ON PARADE
Ray Mason

I went on a holiday to the USA in 1987, touring with a basketball buddy. We ended up in New Orleans in time for the big parade, only to find the 'Big Easy' wasn't as easy as they made out.

While we were watching the parade, we decided to have a quiet beer, only to find out to our amazement that it was illegal to have bottles or cans on the street.

We received this news from a friendly policeman who proceeded to take us into custody. Despite protesting our innocence and our ignorance of the law, it wasn't until we reached the police station that we were able to convince someone of the depth of our plight.

The desk sergeant realised that we were Australian tourists and took pity on us, letting us off with a warning and even offering to try to make amends. He was surprised when we declined his offer of buying us a drink.

RASKOLS
Garry Williamson

I arrived in PNG in 1990 for a three-year contract. I enjoyed running and have always enjoyed a beer. Through work I met people from Hash House Harriers, a worldwide social running group. Beer consumption played a big part in the social activities. That didn't scare me, but the price of beer over there did.

I soon discovered that the way around this problem was to brew my own. I managed to put a kit together and put down my first brew.

A few weeks later I was having trouble sleeping so I decided to watch TV. It was 2.30 a.m. and I was starting to doze off.

Suddenly I was startled by a series of loud bangs followed by the sound of breaking glass. The house alarms were ringing and the dogs were barking.

I was quickly in a state of absolute panic and was lying on the floor trying to turn off the television and the lights.

I thought the local Raskol gangs were raiding the place. I figured they had let off some shots and would soon be coming over the eight-foot barbed wire fences.

Then I had another thought: The Beer.

I went to the back window, looked out cautiously and saw the majority of my first brewing effort running across the patio with glass strewn amongst it. My money-saving exercise had exploded in the most spectacular way.

The next Monday night that the Harriers met I was given a mug of beer to skol for wasting beer. After a few tips my following efforts were more successful and less stressful.

RUSSIAN LIGHTS
Paul Egan

During my tour of Europe in 1990, I promised myself to try a local beer at every overnight stop — not an arduous task at all.

I settled down to a meal at a restaurant in Moscow and, as was my custom, asked the waiter for a local beer. He offered me typical black market goods — caviar, watches, military items — but seemed reluctant to bring me beer.

I persisted. I had been looking forward to a beer; it had been a full day touring and I was parched. 'Light beer,' I said, with my best Russian accent.

'Will you buy watch?' asked my entrepreneurial waiter — and I agreed.

That did the trick.

He brought to the table a 500ml bottle of Baltika No 9, which I thought was by far the finest light beer I'd tried. So good that I ordered three more. More than satisfied with my waiter's recommendation and in such a jolly mood, I purchased about $270 of the black market goods from him.

He too was obviously happy and shouted me one for the road.

Later I told our State tour guide that the waiter had put me on to this great light beer, but that it had a kick to it. I probably sounded a little Russian at that stage.

Boris the State tour guide (I kid you not) looked at the bottle, gave me a wry smile and told me that it was light in colour only — it had an alcohol content of eight per cent and then some!

I look back on that night with fond (if a little hazy) memories and to this day I have my Russian mementos (worth about ten dollars) as a reminder.

I drink to make other people interesting.

George Jean Nathan

THE TASTE TEST
Maurice Kealy

During the early 1960s, I was living and working in London as well as playing Rugby Union for the famous London Irish Rugby Club. One evening, a representative from a major brewing company knocked on my door, inquiring about my level of beer consumption as well as choice of brand.

On learning my preferences towards beer, I was asked if I would be interested in taking part in a beer sampling study.

WOULD I WHAT?!?

I was informed that each week a representative from the brewing establishment would deliver twelve large bottles of different beer for myself and selected others to sample. The bottles came unmarked except that each had been inscribed with a letter ranging from A to L.

The task was simple. Drink the stuff and on the accompanying sheet mark the beers for levels of taste, clarity, colour and aroma, as well as the all-important alcoholic content.

Every Saturday the 'free liquid amber' was duly delivered to my abode and subsequently stored for later consumption. Of course, rugby was the usual agenda of the day (as was partaking in a beverage or two), and the after-match functions were always quite boisterous. As anybody from the era and area (Sunbury on Thames) would know, some of the times had in Fitzy's bar (The Nissan Hut) were quite an event.

The Rugby Club had built a new stand and bar; however, the concrete monstrosity lacked the atmosphere and heart of a good old London bar. The cold and impersonal stand and bar lay dormant as the parties raged on at Fitzy's till the wee hours.

Few of the boys owned cars (let alone were able to drive them) so we all had to bum a lift back to North London. The chosen few were invited back to my place for a glass or two of the free stuff, and after all the singing (which invariably included a few Welsh hymns) and dancing (especially after a match against the

London Welsh) a drink or two were needed to quench the thirst.

In the words of the great Mr Bazza McKenzie we were all 'as dry as a pommie's towel'. And thus the sampling began. As you can imagine, six large Irish lads sampling and studying the finer points of this peculiar drop was a sight to behold (especially at two o'clock in the morning).

Needless to say, I had to spend the rest of the week filling out the form that had accompanied the brew. Hours and hours were spent calculating the high and low points of the flavour, fizz and nose of the last week's batch.

This frightful experience continued for twelve straight weeks. Handing back the empties, picking up the new and swapping over the information sheets was thirsty work, so as every Saturday rolled by, so did the chosen ones, to participate in tasting the new week's batch.

As word spread of our existence, the offers for lifts back up to NW2 (North London) became as common as the brew we had to pay for. However, as I was true to my friends, it was still the usual bunch who had the arduous job of polishing off twelve of the best each Saturday night (or perhaps Sunday morning).

It became obvious that our hard work had not gone unnoticed as the unnamed company came to the party, offering me another twelve weeks of their lager, which today has become one of the most popular lagers on the market.

Unfortunately — or fortunately — the rugby season had by this time passed so I was forced to drink the gold on my own. However, each time I decide that I might have a drop of the great stuff, it brings back some of the greatest memories of my time back in the Old Dart.

JOKES

Did you hear the one about the manager of a brewery whose sales were not as good as they could be? If the truth be known, nobody liked the beer.

Anyway, this executive decided that marketing was the way to sell more and he hired Brett Whiteley to paint a new picture that would encapsulate everything that was modern and cutting-edge about the beer.

Dear old Brett scratched a little and then came up with his painting of a couple going hammer and tongs on Bondi Beach.

Brett said nobody could see the picture until the company's big PR launch.

The manager got everybody together for the big event and the painting was unveiled.

'What the hell does that have to do with my beer?' asked the executive on seeing the work.

'Well,' said Brett with a laugh. 'It's f——ing close to water.'

You heard about the brewery worker who fell into the vat of beer and drowned?

At the inquest the coroner thanked the man's colleagues for doing their best to save him and told the family it was a terrible tragedy but at least their relative died a quick death.

'Be buggered,' yelled one of his mates. 'It was a very slow death. He got out to piss three times.'

You heard about the blokes out fishing in a dinghy off the coast of Tasmania? One of them got his line snagged on something heavy and after a battle he pulled up a treasure chest. In the chest was an Arabian lamp, the sort that has genies in it.

So, the guy gives it a rub and, you guessed it, out pops a genie.

The genie perches on the bow and cuts to the chase.

'You've got one wish, get to it quick because I don't like it out here and I especially don't like boats.'

The fishermen are somewhat taken aback by the genie's demeanour and are disappointed that it is a bloke; nonetheless, one of the blokes has a bright idea and announces that he wishes the sea was made of beer.

Before you know it the genie is gone, the sea is a frothing mass of amber liquid and his mate is furious.

'You idiot,' he yells. 'Now we're going to have to pee in the boat!'

This bear walks into a pub and asks the mean-faced barmaid — a real bar bitch — for a beer.

'Sorry, mate,' she says. 'Don't serve people without shoes on. Bugger off.'

So the bear gets up and walks out but is back in a few minutes with a pair of shoes on. He sits at the table and asks the mean-faced barmaid for a beer.

'Look, you've got shoes on and that's good, but you ain't wearing a shirt so bugger off, there's no beer for you,' she says.

So the bear goes out and comes back in a tuxedo, with a top hat and nice shoes, and thinks to himself that this time the mean-faced barmaid can't possibly refuse him service.

'Can I have a beer now?' he says.

'No,' says the barmaid. 'To tell you the truth I can't stand bears.'

So the bear stands up, rips her head off and eats her.

Wiping the blood off his chin he walks up to the manager and says, 'Get me a bloody beer right now!'

'Sorry, mate,' says the manager. 'Can't serve people who take drugs.'

'Never taken a drug in my life,' says the frustrated and confused bear.

'Oh yeah?' says the manager. 'What about that barbituate?'

These three blokes have been out working on a building site all day when they decide to go for a beer. Unfortunately the local has been yuppified and the bouncer tells them they can't come in because they aren't wearing ties.

One of them pulls off his sock, ties it around his neck and fronts the bouncer again who lets him in.

The other grabs the belt from his trousers, ties it around his neck and he's let in.

The last bloke hasn't got socks or a belt so he runs back to the car and grabs the jumper leads and ties them around his neck.

The bouncer looks at him and says, 'You can come in, but don't go starting anything!'

This bloke walks into a bar and says to the barmaid, 'I'll have a schooner of lager, thanks.' He pays his money, knocks back the whole lot in one hit, burps and bellows 'Piss' before walking out.

Two days later he orders the same thing, goes through the same ritual and yells 'Piss' again as he leaves.

The next day the manager is waiting for him and before the bloke can order, the manager says, 'Piss off.'

'No problem,' says the man. 'I'll have a schooner of your ale then.'

Two little boys decide that they want to be like Dad. They both decide they will ask Mum for a beer and learn to swear. One gets the idea to say bloody while the other says shit.

So, when Mum comes into the room and asks them what they want the first says, 'I'll have a bloody beer,' and is duly beaten and sent to bed.

The second boy is then asked what he wants.

'Shit, I don't know, anything but a beer,' he says.

I know I'm drinking myself to a slow death, but then I'm in no hurry.

Robert Benchley

A bear walks into a bar.

    Barman: 'What can I get you?'

    Bear: 'I'll have a schooner of ... beer.'

    Barman: 'Why the big pause?'

    Bear: 'Dunno. I was just born with them.'

A recent study has found that hormones in beer can turn a man into a woman.

In a controlled situation a group of men were forced to drink fifteen schooners a day. Each put on weight, talked too much, stopped making sense, argued over nothing, became emotional, weren't interested in sex and had accidents in shopping centre car parks.

Did you hear about the alcoholic who got caught stealing twenty-two beers from a bottle shop?

When dragged before the magistrate he said he should be let off because there wasn't enough evidence.

'What do you mean?' asked the magistrate.

'Well,' he said, 'if I'd taken twenty-four they'd have a case, but I'm not that stupid.'

A particularly drunk bloke was walking home from the pub one night when he found himself near the local church. He entered and sat down in the confessional.

The priest waited for him to start confessing but the man just groaned, so the priest coughed to get his attention. This didn't work, so he banged on the grille.

'No use banging on the door, mate, there's no paper in here either,' said the drunk.

A couple of blokes were lost up in the snowfields and sure they were about to die. All of a sudden a kelpie came bounding over the pass with a small keg of beer around his neck, in much the same fashion as the famous St Bernards of the European Alps.

'Look at that,' said one of the blokes. 'Man's best friend has come to our rescue.'

'Yeah,' said the other. 'I think the dog wants to help too.'

A baby seal walks into a bar and orders a schooner of New.

The barman says that he doesn't get too many beer-drinking seals in his pub.

'Well, we're not about to order a bloody Canadian Club on the rocks, are we?' says the seal.

Which reminds me of the baby seal that walked into a club.

Then there was this dingo that walks into an outback pub and orders a beer.

The barmaid thinks she'll get the bludger back for the crimes of his relatives and demands $50 for the drink.

The dingo pays and then she says, 'You know, we don't get many dingoes around here.'

'At $50 a beer I'm not that surprised,' he says.

Q. Why do elephants drink?
A. To forget.

Q. Why do Queenslanders call their beer XXXX?
A. They can't spell beer.

Q. Why do Queenslanders call their beer XXXX?
A. They can't count to five.

There was this bloke who came from outback Queensland and he hits the big smoke, parking his ute outside a pub where he knows his mate's sister works.

He walks in and orders a beer and starts up a conversation with the girl.

They get talking and he pumps her for some information on what to do in the city.

She tells him about a couple of good restaurants and clubs and the like, but he seems nervous about going out by himself.

He then asks her to come out with him, but she's a city chick and he's a real bushie and she doesn't want to be seen out with him so she says no.

The bloke has obviously misread the girl.

Then he says, 'Listen, how about coming out with me tonight? I'll shout you dinner and the like and because it's been such a good year on the farm I'll give you $200 for your time.'

She doesn't want to, but thinks she could do with the money and so they go out and have a pretty good time, but she makes it clear that he'd better not get any fancy ideas.

The bloke then says that he's desperate for some, having spent so long on the farm that even the sheep have begun to look cute. He offers to chip in $300 for her time.

The girl has had a few and could do with the money so she figures why not, so they go back to her place and do it.

Afterwards she asks where exactly he's from and is amazed to find he's from the same farm as her brother.

'Wait until I tell him I met you,' she says.

'Yeah,' says the bloke. 'And make sure you tell him I gave you that $500 he owed ya.'

A young Kiwi bloke decides he's going to settle in Oz. Eager to fit in, he decides to forget about sheep and go along with the local customs.

The first night here he goes to a pub and meets a couple of regulars who get him pretty pissed. They then decide to have some fun.

'Mate, I'll give you $1000 if you let me smash a dozen full beer bottles over your head,' says one of them.

'I don't think so,' says the Kiwi, getting a bit nervous.

'C'mon, mate,' the rest of them say. 'We've all had a shot at this. It's part of Australian culture.'

'Well,' says the Kiwi. 'If it's a local custom I'll give it a shot. I've got a hard head and I could do with the money.'

So the local gets the dozen bottles and begins to smash them over the Kiwi's head.

It hurts like hell and there's blood dripping down the bloke's face but he hangs in there for the first eleven.

Then the Australian stops, opens the last bottle and walks away while swigging it back.

The Kiwi asks him what's going on.

'Well, I'm not a complete fool,' says the Australian. 'If I smashed this one it'd cost me $1000.'

This bloke walks into a bar and orders two beers. He sits down at an empty table, drinks one and pours the other on his hand.

He does this a couple of times before the barman asks what he's up to.

The guy blushes and then says, 'I'm just getting me date drunk before we go home.'

This flea walks into an empty bar, jumps up onto the stool and yells to the barman, 'Hey, mate, get us a beer would ya?'

The barman thinks he hears something but can't see anyone so he walks away.

The flea gets cranky and jumps up onto the bar and yells, 'Mate, get me a bloody beer. I'm dying of thirst!'

The barman looks down and sees the cranky flea, shakes his head and then gets the little bugger a beer.

The flea throws the beer up in the air, does a somersault and lands on his feet just as the beer pours out right into his mouth. He skols the lot and doesn't spill a drop.

'Another one, thanks, mate,' says the flea after letting out a rather large belch.

So the barman gets him another and the flea does exactly the same thing.

He does this time and again until he's run out of money and then the little bugger jumps off the bar and says goodbye.

The barman is still wondering if he hasn't dreamt the whole thing when the flea weaves his way back in.

'I thought you were going home,' says the barman.

'I would be, but some bastard stole me bloody dog,' says the flea.

This bloke's been at the pub all night and is totally tanked when the barman tells him to go home and sleep it off. After a bit of an argument and a little sulking the guy says, 'Well, bugger you then, I'll take my custom somewhere else!'

He gets off the stool and falls flat on his face. People rush to help him up but he tells them to 'bugger off' and tries to do it himself.

'God, I'm more pissed than I thought,' he thinks and giving up on the idea of standing he drags himself across the floor and to the door where he falls down the few steps to the footpath.

'I'll just lie here and get some fresh air,' he thinks, but even that doesn't work because every time he drags himself upright he falls down again.

Fortunately he only lives a few houses up the street so he just drags himself along until he gets to his front door.

Reaching up for the door knob he drags himself up so he can get the key in the lock and again falls down on his face.

Giving up on walking he drags himself down the hall, up onto the bed and next to his wife who mutters in her sleep about smelling like a brewery, being out all night, the dinner going cold and all that trivial stuff.

Before she can get a head of steam up the guy is asleep and so is she.

The next morning the missus wakes him early and starts again.

'You must've really tied one on last night,' she says.

'What makes you say that?' says the bloke whose head is hosting a private show by AC/DC.

'Well, the pub rang this morning and said you'd left your wheelchair behind again,' she says.

A drunk is making a bit of trouble in a pub so the barman decides to toss him out and bar him until he is sober.

The drunk weaves his way out the door and wanders around the corner where he finds another door so he goes in and orders a beer.

'I told you to go home,' said the barman.

The drunk is quite taken aback.

'How many frigging pubs do you own?' he spits on his way out.

A group of blokes are drinking in a pub when an old drunk comes up to one of them, stabs his finger in the guy's chest and says, 'Your mum is the best root north of the Mildura.'

Everyone thinks there's going to be a fight, but the bloke just ignores the drunk and turns to order another drink.

The old soak staggers off, only to return a little while later and confront the bloke again.

'I gave your mum one this morning and boy was she hot!'

The bloke gets angry but turns away without replying and the drunk weaves off across the bar again.

Sure enough, he's back again a few minutes later.

'Your mum gives the best ...' Before he can finish the bloke explodes. 'For God's sake go home, Dad, you're drunk!'

Two mates were out on the turps having a pretty good night. They'd known each other since school days and even though one was university educated and the other was barely literate they got on pretty well.

The smart guy says he'd like to go out and maybe have a bit of slap and tickle.

'Good,' says the slower one. 'I know this bloody great club where you go in, have a couple of beers on the house, then go upstairs with whoever's arrived, have a root, go back down, have a couple more beers until somebody else arrives, then you go upstairs and have another root and so on until you've had your fill. Then when ya leave they pay ya.'

'I find that a little hard to believe,' says the smart one.

'Oh, it's true all right,' says his mate.

'Well, have you been there?' asks the other.

'Nah, but me sister has.'

A family from the mountains of New Zealand decided after their twelfth child that they had enough children and maybe it was time to stop. Not knowing what to do, they went to the doctor and were told that the bloke could have a vasectomy.

After being told exactly what that was, the father of twelve decided he wasn't too keen on the idea. He asked the doctor if there was another option.

The doctor said they could stop having sex, but the wife was concerned that this might lead to problems.

Condoms were out because neither knew how to use them.

So the doctor suggested a method that had worked for Tasmanian hill families for many generations.

He told the man to go home, put a cracker in an empty can of beer, hold it in his left hand and count to ten.

The man said he couldn't see how such a thing would stop him having children but figured the doctor knew what he was talking about.

He went home that night and went out the backyard where he lit a cracker, put it in the can in his right hand and began to count.

2 3 4 5 ...

Momentarily confused, he paused, then put the can between his legs and continued to count on the other hand.

7 8 9 10 ...

Vasect Oh Me Oh My ... that smarts!

A couple of very drunk old boys are sitting at a bar in one of the bohemian parts of the big city — one of those places where the men wear earrings and shave their heads and the women wear boots, shave nothing and roll their own.

Anyway, there's one of these urban girls sitting next to the old guys and she's wearing the standard uniform: singlet top, hairy armpits, torn jeans and boots.

The two men get friendly with the girl and figure she's all right and tell her just to signal the barman any time she wants a beer and it's on them.

So the girl raises her arm and the barman runs over and gets her a beer and this goes on for half the night: she raises her arm, gets a beer and the old guys pay.

The old guys are blotto by the time it comes for a last drink.

'Get the ballet dancer something from the top shelf,' says one.

'Ballet dancer?' says the girl quizzically.

'Well, anyone who can get their leg up high enough to order a beer musht be shome short of dancer,' says the drunk old man.

Have you heard the one about the three pieces of string who decide they want to experience the good life inside a pub?

The first two slick themselves down, straighten themselves up and walk up to the bar and ask for a beer.

'Sorry,' says the barman. 'We don't serve string around here.'

The third has hung back, and hearing that he figures he might try a different approach. He twists himself round into a knot and frays his ends before walking to the bar.

The barman is not impressed.

'Hey, I told your friends we don't serve string here; you are a piece of string, aren't you?' he says.

'Nah, I'm a frayed knot,' comes the reply.

There's a smart alec bloke at a pub who reckons he can tell any beer in a blind test.

So they put a blindfold on him and start bringing out different beers.

Boags, VB, James Squire ... he picks them all until one wag comes out of the toilet with a glass of urine and puts it before him.

'That's p-p-p-piss,' splutters the smart alec.

'I know,' says the wag. 'But whose piss is it?'

Three businessmen meet in Sydney to discuss projections for the international company for the next financial year. One is from America, one from England and one is an Aussie.

After crunching numbers, planning mass sackings and boosting their executive entitlements the trio head for the nearest bar to wash out their mouths.

'I'll get you three local beers, eh?' says the Australian.

'Naw,' says the Yank. 'I'll have a Bud.'

'I'd prefer a pint of bitter,' says the Pom.

The Aussie turns around and asks for a pint of bitter, a Bud and a lemonade.

The others ask him why he hasn't ordered a beer.

'Well, if you're not drinking beer neither am I,' says the Aussie.

A drunk walks into a bar and takes the last bar stool right next to a rather proper old gal who's drinking a glass of wine.

The drunk orders a beer but soon the lady notices a terrible smell.

She turns to him and says, 'Excuse me, but I think you've pooped in your pants.'

'I shertainly have,' says the drunk.

'Well, why don't you run off and clean yourself up then?' says the lady.

'Yeah, yeah, I will, it's just that I haven't finished yet.'

A drunk walks into a pub and says to the bartender that he wants a beer but he's got no money.

The bloke tells him to bugger off.

'Hang on,' says the drunk. 'What if I show you a trick?'

'Well, it'd better be good,' says the bartender.

'Oh, it's good, in fact it's so good I think you should give me two beers.'

'We'll see,' says the bartender.

So the drunk carefully reaches into his pocket and draws out a green frog and places it on the bar. He then reaches into his other pocket and pulls out a miniature piano which he places in front of the frog.

The bartender is amazed, but even more so when the little critter starts to bang out the hottest jazz tunes he's ever heard.

Sure enough, the bartender shouts the drunk two beers.

When he's finished these, the drunk asks, 'If I can top that will you give me free beer for the rest of the night?'

'If you can top that you can have free beer for the rest of the week,' says the bartender, thinking that the pub will be packed with people coming to see the amazing jazz-playing frog.

The drunk smiles to himself and reaches into his pocket and pulls out a lady rat in a slinky dress. The rat leaps from his hand, leans against the piano and sings along.

The bartender is blown away and keeps his word. While the drunk drinks, the rat and frog entertain customers and the pub is packed every night.

On the last night of their deal a theatrical agent walks in and cannot believe what he sees.

He immediately offers the drunk $1000 for the frog and the rat.

'Nah, forget it,' says the drunk.

The agent then says he'll give $1000 for the rat alone.

'You're on,' says the drunk.

The agent takes the rat and leaves, but the bartender is furious.

'You just broke up a million dollar duet for a lousy $1000!' he yells.

'Don't worry about it,' says the drunk. 'The frog's a ventriloquist.'

This old geezer's lying on his deathbed, family gathered around and everyone is feeling a bit emotional.

Even his nagging wife is in a good mood.

'You've been a good husband,' she says. 'We've had a good life together. Is there anything I can get you, love? Any last request?'

'I don't want to be any trouble,' he says.

'Oh, sweetheart,' she replies. 'Everybody deserves a last wish. You just ask and I'll do my best.'

'Well, I would love one of those beers you put in the back fridge yesterday,' he says.

'Oh my God,' she says. 'Just like you — selfish and thoughtless. Those are for the wake!'

They who drink beer will think beer.

Washington Irving

This drunk walks into a bar and says to the bartender, 'Give me a beer before the shit hits the fan.'

The bartender gives him a drink and walks off.

The drunk calls him over again and says, 'Give me another beer before the shit hits the fan.'

The bartender obliges and this goes on for a while before the bartender says, 'I hope you've got enough money to pay for these.'

'Oops, the shit's hit the fan,' says the drunk.

A Queensland cow cockie parks his ute outside a Sydney pub, grabs his swag and shotgun out of the back, goes inside, puts the gear down and has a big afternoon on the beer.

Towards evening he picks up his swag and shotgun and leaves, only to return a few seconds later red with anger.

He lets off a shot into the ceiling and yells, 'Somebody has stole me frigging ute and if it's not back by the time I finish me next beer I'm gonna have to do what I did in Melbourne!'

The locals pick the bits of ceiling from their receding hair and look at each other nervously.

The bartender gets the cow cockie a beer and starts to sweat when he notices the car park still empty.

'Will you tell me what happened in Melbourne?' asks the bartender.

'Yeah, I will,' the cockie says. 'I had to walk all the way home.'

A wombat emerges from a building site and walks across the road into a pub and asks for a beer.

The bartender is taken aback to find a talking wombat.

They get chatting and the bartender asks where the wombat works.

'Over the road on the building site,' comes the reply.

'Well, you know with your skills you could get a job in the circus,' says the bartender.

'A circus?' asks the wombat.

'Yes, a circus,' says the bartender.

'One of those joints with tents, animals and sawdust?' asks the wombat.

'That's the one,' says the bartender.

'What would a frigging plasterer do at a circus?' asks the wombat.

A greyhound has just ordered a beer from the bar and is walking back to his seat when he overhears a group of racehorses talking.

'You know, I was at Flemington yesterday and the strangest thing happened,' says one. 'I was ambling along at the back of the pack, getting those bastard owners back for chopping off my you-know-whats, when all of a sudden I felt this red hot sensation up my dot like somebody had shoved a burning poker up it. Next thing I know I'm four lengths in front and I've set the bloody race record.'

'Same thing happened to me,' says another

horse. 'I was at Randwick right at the back of the field when all of a sudden I got this incredible burning penetration up me bum and before you know it I'd won the race.'

The third says that the same thing had happened to a couple of his mates.

The greyhound then chips in and says, 'Sorry to intrude, guys, but exactly the same thing happened to me when I was racing a fortnight ago. I was coming last as usual, thinking they'd have to retire me after this effort, when all of a sudden I got that red hot poker feeling up me out chute and whammo I've won the bloody race.'

The horses all went silent, so the greyhound continued on to his table.

'Can you believe that?' said the horses when he'd gone. 'A talking greyhound!'

Three English backpackers were in a bar and spotted an Irishman among the locals.

One lad said he was going to get this guy worked up. He walked over to the Irishman and said to him, 'Hey, mate, your St Patrick was a bastard and a wanker.'

The Irishman put down his drink and the Pom backed off a bit, but then the bloke just turned away and said, 'Oh really, didn't know that. There ya go.'

The Englishman walked back to his mates quite crestfallen. 'I told him St Patrick was a right bastard and he didn't seem to care!'

'I'll show you how it's done,' the second Pom said and walked over and tapped the Irishman on the shoulder. 'I hear your St Patrick was a gay homosexual.'

The Irishman again put his drink down, thought for a second and replied, 'Oh, I didn't know that, there you go.'

The Pom walked back to his mates and said he couldn't get a rise out of him.

The third Pom decided he had the right stuff and told his mates to watch his form.

'I hear your St Patrick was an Englishman!' he said to the Irishman who replied almost immediately, 'Yeah, that's what your friends were trying to tell me.'

Which reminds me of the old joke about the Aussie, the Pom and the Scot. All three were drinking a beer outside in a beer garden when three flies flew down and landed in the beer.

The Pom said, 'I'm not drinking this, it's got germs in it.'

The Aussie just picked the fly out and kept drinking, while the Scot pulled his fly out by the wings and said, 'Spit it back, you wee thievin' laddie.'

An Irish bloke walks into a bar one Friday and asks for three beers. The bartender serves him and then watches as the bloke takes a sip from one glass, then another and then another, until he has finished all three.

The Irishman then goes back and orders three more.

The curious bartender asks him why he doesn't drink one at a time like everybody else.

The Irishman tells him that he's got a brother in Australia and one in America and they made a pact that on this day every year they would go to a pub in their respective parts of the world and drink a round or two to remember when they were together. It seems that they had been very close and had a drink every Friday since they were eighteen.

So, the Irishman comes back every Friday and does the same thing and everybody in the pub becomes acquainted with the strange ritual.

Then one Friday the bloke comes in and only orders two drinks.

There's much speculation in the bar about why he's done this and everybody feels a bit sorry for him, thinking one of his brothers must have died.

The barman walks up and passes on their feelings, but the Irishman just smiles and says not to worry.

'Nobody has died,' he says. 'It's just that I've joined AA and don't drink any more.'

A father and his underage son were sitting in the pub one day having a drink and the old man was teaching the young bloke a little bit about drinking etiquette.

'A gentleman never drinks too much,' said his dad, who had had quite a few himself. 'It brings shame on the family and loss of face.'

'How can you tell if you've drunk too much?' asked the young bloke.

'Well,' said the old man. 'You see those two women over there? If you had disgraced yourself with the drink you would see four.'

'But, Father ... there's only one lady sitting over there,' said the son.

This bloke gets rotten drunk one night at the pub and can't get his keys out of his pocket when he gets home.

Fumbling around, he spills all the coins onto the doorstep before finally getting the key out.

He's too drunk to pick them up and figures he'll get them in the morning, but when the sun comes up he is woken by his wife who yells out, 'Come and look at this, the milkman has left twenty-two cartons of milk here!'

A bloke walks into a country pub and sees a sign with the letters WYBMADIITY above the bar. Confused and intrigued, he asks the barman what the letters stand for.

Barman replies: 'Will you buy me a drink if I tell you?'

Bloke says: 'Sure, but what do the letters stand for?'

Barman again replies: 'Will you buy me a drink if I tell you?'

Bloke says: 'I said that I would, so what is it?'

Barman replies: 'Will you buy me a drink if I tell you?'

Bloke says: 'Yeah, yeah, just tell me what the letters stand for.'

Barman replies: 'Will you buy me a drink if I tell you?'

Bloke says: 'You're a bloody broken record with bad hearing. What is it?'

Barman replies: 'Will you buy me a drink if I tell you?'

Bloke says: 'I give up.'

And then the barman came clean and explained to the bloke what WYBMADIITY means ... again.

A shearer walks into a pub and says, 'Give me a f——ing beer.'

The barmaid says she will not be spoken to like that and refuses to serve him.

'Look, lady, I don't give a flying f——k what you think, just give me a f——ing beer!'

Again she says that she will not serve him if he uses language like that.

'For f——k's sake, I want a f——ing beer, right f——ing now or else!'

The barmaid takes a deep breath and says she is going to show him some manners. She tells him to get behind the bar and she will show him how to order a beer.

They swap places and the woman says, 'Excuse me, kind sir, could I have a beer, please?'

'No, you can go and get f——d,' says the shearer. 'You wouldn't give me a f——ing beer, so f—k off!'

Two Victorians had popped up to southern New South Wales for a holiday and found themselves in a shearer's bar staring at this big bloke opposite them.

The barman noticed their fascination and warned them not to look at the man because he hated people staring and had a foul temper.

Still, the southerners could not take their eyes off the guy and sure enough he came stomping over to them, red-faced and furious.

'What the f—k do you think you're looking at?' he demanded.

'Ah, nothing,' said one before adding nervously, 'it's your perfect teeth, I have never seen such perfect teeth.'

'Yeah, well, they are nice, but stop staring or

I'll rip your head off,' said the big bloke before going back to his beer.

Unfortunately the two Victorians continued to stare, unable to look at anything else for too long.

The big bloke came stomping over again.

'I told you, now you're going to get it!' he bellowed.

'No, wait,' said the one who had commented on his teeth. 'It's just that you, well, you have great teeth, but your eyes are even better. They are the most amazing eyes.'

'Yeah, they're pretty good,' said the big man coyly.

'Bet you have never worn glasses,' said the Victorian.

'Nah,' said the big bloke.

It was then that the other Victorian, feeling more comfortable with the situation, decided to put his two bob worth in.

'Nah, you would never need glasses with eyes like that, so who cares if there's nothing for them to hang on to.'

A woman drove me to drink and I didn't even have the decency to thank her.

WC Fields

A big, bulky abattoir worker called Bob was renowned for his love of beer and the quantities he could consume.

The bloke was a legend in the small Hunter Valley town where he lived and was said to put away about twenty schooners a day.

One day he took a bit crook and was talked into visiting the local doctor for a check-up.

The doc asked him the usual questions and then got onto his lifestyle.

'Do you smoke?' asked the doc.

'Nah, mate,' said Bob proudly.

'What about the grog?' asked the doc.

'Yeah, mate, might have a few,' said Bob.

'How many?' asked the doc.

'Geez, I dunno,' said Bob.

'Well, how many would you have in a day?' asked the doc.

'Ahhhh ... it's hard to say,' said Bob.

'A couple of schooners?' asked the doc.

'Well ...' squirmed Bob.

'Five?' the doc persisted.

'Mmm ...' the big fella said.

'Bob, if you're drinking more than five schooners a day you're drinking far too much,' the doctor warned.

'For f—k's sake, doc, give a man a break. I'd f——ing well spill more than that!' exclaimed Bob while taking his leave.

Peter Lalor is one of those fortunate individuals who has managed to reconcile his love of beer with the need to earn a wage.

He has worked and drunk his way around the world as a journalist, eventually managing to erase any dividing line between beer and journalism. In mid-1998 he began to write a weekly and extremely popular column for *The Daily Telegraph* in Sydney, succinctly titled 'Beer'.

In 2001 he added the 'Bar Reviews' to his CV and now describes himself as a workaholic who is hard at it twenty-four seven, as they say. If he's not at the computer, he's at the bar and if he's not at either then he's at home with his wife, Sue, and two children, Lucy and Harry.

The proudest moments in his life are as follows. The time two-year-old Lucy asked her dad if she could get him another beer from the fridge and the day Harry announced the pub was more fun than the playground.

Peter is a professional storyteller with the gift of the gab, especially when lubricated by his favourite beverage. He discovered over the years that many of *The Daily Telegraph* readers are similarly skilled and decided to combine their tales with some of his own for your reading pleasure.

He wishes to thank everybody who contributed to this book and warns some that he has handed their stories on to the authorities and either the police or health authorities will be in touch with them. You know who you are.

Sue did the hard yards coordinating the project and reminding Peter that he should try and stick to the English language.

Harry and Lucy were no help at all, although they have contributed greatly to Peter and Sue's need for beer and humour.

Peter is now the Chief Cricket Writer for *The Australian* and its Beer Editor.